KEEP

YOUR FMOUTH

SHUT

Frontispiece:

NO DREAM IS TOO BIG

This book, penned without the weight of experience, contains both imperfections and potential. Listen closely, for its message echoes across time and circumstance: **Do not tarry for the elusive perfect moment.** The sands of opportunity slip through our fingers, and the hourglass of destiny waits for no one.

Today—that humble canvas upon which we paint our aspirations—is the fertile ground where dreams take root. It matters not if you harbor ambitions of birthing a company, weaving tales into books, composing melodies that dance upon the air, or conjuring cinematic magic. The genesis lies in the present, where intention meets action.

Set a due date, my friend. Mark it on your soul's calendar. Let it be a beacon, a North Star guiding your endeavors. Without a deadline, dreams languish in the nebulous realm of "someday." But with a date etched in ink, you summon the forces of commitment and urgency.

And now, a whispered secret: **Keep your mouth shut.** Guard your vision like a dragon hoards its treasure. Share it selectively, for not all ears are tuned to the symphony of your heart's desires. Speak only to those who fan the flames, who whisper encouragement into the winds of uncertainty.

But remember this: Silence alone does not birth dreams. **Action**—that tireless blacksmith—shapes raw ideas into reality. Roll up your sleeves, wield your tools, and forge progress. Inch by inch, keystroke by keystroke, brushstroke by brushstroke, weave the tapestry of your destiny.

So, my fellow dreamer, heed these words: **No dream is too big.** The cosmos conspires in your favor, awaiting your bold strokes upon the canvas of existence. The curtain rises; the stage awaits. Step into the spotlight, and let your dreams unfurl like banners in the wind.

For today, my friend, is the day you begin.

- **Copyright Page**

Glossary

Calate: kid or teenager

Ofrenda: is a **ritual display** placed on a home altar during the annual and traditionally Mexican **Día de los Muertos** celebration

Calaberita: type of pumpkin for the Day of the Deads in Mexico

Why do you have to shut your mouth every time you can?

"A fish with his mouth shut avoids the hook."

If you have the answer to that question, it is probably because you had a situation where just keeping your mouth shut would be better than it was. We talk to show our presence or to feel important in front of people.

Silence will take you to magical places you couldn't get before just because you didn't know how to shut your mouth. Sometimes, you probably think your opinion is needed, but believe me, it is usually useless and can lead you to a situation you won't like.

TABLE OF CONTENTS

CHAPTER 1: ……………………….AT WORK

CHAPTER 2: ……………………….IN A RELATIONSHIP

CHAPTER 3:……………………….AT THE GYM

CHAPTER 4:……………………….AT SCHOOL

CHAPTER 5: ……………………….YOUR NEXT MOVE

CHAPTER 6: ……………………….MAKING MONEY $$$

CHAPTER 7: ……………………….YOUR ACHIEVEMENTS

CHAPTER 8: ……………………….YOUR FEELINGS

CHAPTER 9: ……………………….YOUR DREAMS

AT WORK 1

"Work hard every day and help others as much as possible."- GEOVANNY ESTRADA

When you tread the well-worn path of toil, your colleagues become companions in the grand theater of enterprise. They say collaboration is the lifeblood of progress—a truth etched on the very stones of the path of wealth. Yet, my tale weaves a different thread, a cautionary note for those who dare dream beyond the mundane. There is a delicate dance between sharing your thoughts and guarding them like precious gems.

Picture me, a humble worker in the sun-kissed plains of South Dakota. The parched earth bore witness to my whispered revelation—an idea, a spark that danced within my mind like a desert mirage. I turned to my coworker, eyes alight, and shared my clandestine plan: "Let us petition our supervisor for a day's bounty of tasks. No respite, no idle moments—just unwavering labor until the sun dips low." So we can go home early today.

My coworker, bless his fickle heart, nodded in agreement. "Geo," he said, "you've struck gold. A shortcut to freedom, a ticket home before dusk." But alas, the winds of betrayal stirred. As he met with our supervisor, he spilled my secret like a clumsy scribe knocking over an inkwell. Their hushed conversation echoed through the corridors:

"Jon," my coworker began, feigning innocence, "can we depart early? Even if our daily burdens are lifted?"

Jon, our stern overseer, fixed him with a gaze as unyielding as the city walls. "Of course not," he thundered. "Why ask the obvious? And Geo—our tireless dreamer—let him toil until the hour of release."

From this, I gleaned a lesson etched in cuneiform upon my soul: **silence is the currency of the wise**. Listen, oh seeker of fortune, and heed these ancient truths:

1. **The Art of Stillness**: Amid the clamor of the marketplace, find solace in quietude. Let your ears drink deep from the well of others' words. For in silence, wisdom blooms like the desert flower after rain.

2. **The Unseen Path**: Not every idea merits proclamation. Guard your musings as a miser guards his gold. Seek counsel, but beware of the bricklayer's advice on gemstones.

3. **The Dance of Balance**: Silence need not shroud your voice forever. When necessity calls, speak boldly and wisely. For even the gods themselves whispered secrets to mortals when the stars aligned.

4. **The Tapestry of Labor**: Work, my friend, is both chisel and canvas. Carve your destiny with diligence, but let joy be your brushstroke. Seek tasks that ignite your spirit, for therein lies true wealth.

And so, dear reader, as the sun kisses the ziggurats and shadows stretch across the Euphrates, remember: **to speak or not to speak—both paths lead to destiny**. Choose wisely,

AT WORK 2

In 2009, after graduating from high school, I tried to get into a civil engineering school for college, but I did not pass the entry-level test, so I couldn't go to college that year. My friends who didn't pass the test at different colleges went to some colleges that did not require to do entry-level tests because everyone could go there, but the careers were limited, so you had to study something you might not want to; most of my friends went there, and they subjected me to go with them because was easy to enter, but I didn't go. Instead of that, I looked for my first full-time job.

Raul was one of my first bosses. The very first was Gera, but Raul was my full-time job boss. He taught me how to work since I didn't know much about growing flowers; he asked me why I wanted to work at his company, flowers. I explained my situation, and he was happy to give me an opportunity there.

Everything was going well until I decided to start sharing part of my dreams with Raul and his brother Pepe. Pepe was a kind of bully who loved to crash on your dreams and make you feel like you would never be good enough for whatever stupid dreams you had. One day, Raul asked me what I wanted to do in life. I responded that I wanted to be a civil engineer and have a lifted truck. Pepe was listening to the conversation and immediately joined us with an extensive and loud laugh followed by a joke: what did you say? He asked me if I could repeat that. And I told him yes, I want to be a civil engineer and have a truck that looks like a monster truck haha haha hahaha he was laughing; the only monster you will have in life is your monster face; you already have a monster face calate and he and Raul were giggling and laughing for that. For so many weeks, I was the reason they laughed.

After that situation, I started thinking that I shouldn't talk about my dreams in the job because that can be dangerous. Unless I want to get bullied or if I don't care that people laugh at me, then it is a good idea to share my stuff with others, but I told myself that I should keep my f mouth shut for the first time.

AT WORK 3

People will not always feel good about your achievements and the success you can achieve in life; at least you have three friends who don't like it when you talk about how your job is outstanding, your boss gives you vacations, and you get a raise. You will think that your family is an exception, but guess what? Nope, you're mistaken if you think it is a good idea to tell your friends and other people how good you are doing at work and let me tell you why.

I was very excited when I started working as an engineer at a big company. After struggling with school for more than five years because I joined the military and my grades were not the best, struggling with classes and work to pay for my rent and food, I met a great professor named Scott. Dr. Scott saw that I struggled to graduate and helped me graduate one semester early. I got my first engineering job and was making money that I had never seen before in my pocket, so I got excited and wanted to share that excitement with my friends and family.

I told my mom that I had a good job and was making good money so she could be happy and not worried for me. I also told my friends, and at first, it seemed like they got happy, but some of them started asking for money, and one said, Hey! Geo, you are making good money now. Can I borrow some from you? I told him that I would like to borrow it, but still, at the moment, I was starting, and I needed to pay some debts; another one gave me advice;

he told me, Hey Geo, I am happy for you that you are making money, but take this advice, keep your mouth shut and don't share what are you making because your friends will start asking for money and if they are having difficulties with money is probably that they won't pay you. You may lose a friend and help all the people you can, but when you try to help someone, they may later see you as a bad person if you ask them for your money back. I took my friend's advice, and I could help some friends without putting them or myself in a situation where we could not be friends anymore, so dear reader, don't share what you are making with too many people.

AT WORK 4

The idea here is that you can keep yourself out of trouble because you cannot control yourself from speaking, either because you are too excited and want to share with others or because you feel pressure at your job. You have to be visible or feel like you are doing your job and feel important.

Some consequences can happen depending on how you talk, not just getting in trouble but also losing what you already have. My mom was working at the hotel and was in a unique program that helps workers with some extra money. Everything was great until here, but after a year, that program was no longer available for the new hires, so they could not get the benefit anymore. My mom was too lovely to share with the new hires that she was getting extra cash. Thank you to this beautiful program, but she didn't know that the program was reset and canceled and was no longer available for the new workers. After sharing this with others, like it is customary in humans to feel jealous that others are getting more than us for apparently doing the job my mom's coworkers when and talked to the manager and said, hey, I want also to be in the program that she is, I also want to get extra cash for the job I'm doing, or we are going to quit because that is not fear to others. The manager tried to explain that it was an old program and was no longer available, but new workers were not happy with that; they wanted everyone to have the same opportunities and benefits so they were treated the same. The manager has to give all employees the same opportunities and benefits, so guess what happens next? The manager removed my mom from that program, and she lost the extra money she was getting just because she was too excited to help others and tell them about how they could also be there.

I don't know if my mom was right when she told others about her benefit program or not, but something I am sure of is that if she hadn't talked about that benefit, she would still have it, so I will let you get your conclusions on this case.

AT WORK 5

Choosing silence over confrontation provides the necessary space for emotions to settle, allowing for a more rational and objective discussion later.

It is easy to get mad when somebody at work orders us to do something or the supervisor acts like the boss and orders us something like hey! Did you finish the report I told you to do last week? Hey, do you have until today to finish the job you are working on? Hey, what are you working on right now? There are some samples of when we have to stay quiet, although we want to replay with a comfortable f you; if you what that shit is done, do it yourself. Yeah, that will feel comfortable, but it is not recommendable if we want to keep our jobs.

I had a boss like that; I think everybody has, had, or will have a boss or a supervisor who, at some point, is going to scream at us and show that he or she is better than us because he/she is either the owner or have a higher position than us right now.

When I was working as an engineer, I thought my supervisor was the worst; every time he came to my office running, trying to surprise me on my phone or not working on the computer so he could start yelling at me that I should be busy all the time even though we were working 12 hours a day, he thought that I should be busy doing something all the time because every minute counts. I believe it is necessary to be productive at work, but some people like to micromanage, which is one of the most stressful things.

My recommendation here is that if you have somebody that irritates you like that at work, don't say anything at the moment, keep your mouth shut, and start looking for a better job because I believe that everyone at any company should be treated with respect, we indeed need money from companies jobs, but companies also need our labor and believe me if you decide to move on and take the risk to work on something that you like, no matter the situation that you are on, things eventually will be better and you will be happier.

AT WORK 6

Have you ever heard the term "think before you speak"? Well, that refers to thinking for one day before you say something you might not like later. In my job as an engineer, I was taking to fill out the silence; this was not always the best move because before I could think before I said something, it was too late. I said things like hey, this job is straightforward, hey, I'm almost done with my tasks for this week. If I say that the job is easy just for my coworkers or in front of the supervisor, they will start thinking well, let's make this guy's job more complicated so he can be happy. The coworkers typically get jealous when they hear that someone is having an easy time at their job or they are enjoying their jobs. They will also find a way to make things more complicated so the person talking like that next time will think before speaking again, or like I want to say; it is just better to keep your f mouth shut and stay out of trouble.

It is usual for people to talk about others, especially at work.

No matter what job you have or what position you are in right now, somebody will come to you telling you how bad or lazy you are or how many problems some person has. Please don't listen to them because this will affect how you see the person. Maybe you like the person they are talking about and could see the person differently after that. Don't be that person who starts talking bad about others to have a conversation, especially if you don't know the person or their problems.

AT WORK 7

If you cannot make friends at work, maybe you are doing something you aren't supposed to. In his book How to Make Friends and Influence People, Dale Carnegie discusses how to make friends when you become interested in others and nobody cares about you or your success at work.

One day, a friend of mine came to me asking if I knew how to make friends at work because, for him, it is complicated. He said nobody likes me at work, and I don't know why; I'm funny and very friendly, but I have problems making friends at work or outside work. I immediately recommended the book "How to Make Friends and Influence People"- by Dale Carnegie, but I also asked him to tell me about his job and how he interacts with people.

His name is George, and this is what work looks like for him. A construction supervisor, George, came early to work in his new pickup truck. He modifies the exhaust to make it louder and ensures that everyone knows how much the new exhaust costs him and how fast his trucks can go. When he shows up to work, everybody knows that he is coming from a mile away because of the noise he makes with the car. Then he says hi to everyone he sees and sometimes makes a bad joke about them. At lunchtime, he jumps in his car and drives to the restaurant for lunch. Finally, he goes around the project to correct their jobs in front of others, saying something like hey

Geo, you should do your job faster; that nail that you put up there is crocked; you are making too much mess with the hammer drill don't you know how to use it?

After seeing him at work, I noticed that he wants a lot of attention, which is one reason people don't like him. People don't care how much your truck costs or how fast it can run. George has no interest in others, and as Dale Carnegie said in his book, it's tough to make friends when we try to impress others; it is more efficient if we get interested in others.

This is what I told George the next week I saw him. George, you need to keep your f mouth shut; people don't have to know how much your truck costs or how fast it can run; if you want to correct others, don't do it in public where everyone can hear that someone is not doing the job correctly. If you want to make friends, get some interest in what others do and show them that you appreciate their job; last, remove the loud exhaust from your truck. Don't try to impress others; instead, ask them how they feel and how you can help them. Make a good impression that you care about others, which will help you make friends.

AT WORK 8-9

Whatever the reason is, staying quiet 90% of the time will bring better results for you.

The goal is to improve your workspace, a complex ecosystem of relationships and diverse personalities. It is crucial to build trust; other coworkers can trust you as you can.

Trust is a cornerstone of effective teamwork. Measuring silence with intentional and thoughtful communication builds trust among colleagues and superiors, fostering a more supportive and collaborative work environment.

Don't tell people how much money you make or tell anybody your paycheck because I'm sure they will not care unless they can benefit from it. If you tell friends, they will probably be more comfortable knowing that you have some extra cash, and they can ask you to borrow some money; borrowing money from friends is very dangerous because it is not only the money, but you also can lose your friendship with them.

While working as an apprentice electrician at college, I was excited to have a job, so I told an excellent friend from high school. She is a lawyer, and her husband is also a lawyer; they were making perfect money, so they bought a new SUV. When I told her about my job, she asked me how much I make. I told her how much I make per hour and compared her salary in Mexico with my salary in the U.S. She thought that I was making more money being an apprentice electrician than she being a lawyer. One day, she asked me if I could borrow money to make a car payment; she complained that work was hard and they were having trouble making car payments. I borrowed her money to make a car payment that month, and she told me it was just for one month. One month passed, and she didn't call me to pay me back. Six months passed, and she never called me. We talked more before I borrowed money to see how we were doing with our lives. She was getting distant as if she didn't want to talk to me anymore; I was sad that we didn't talk anymore, not for the money. After one year, I texted her, "Hey friend, how are you doing? Is everything ok? Can you pay me my money now? It is over a year, and you told me it was just for one month. She replied that she would pay me but didn't want me to text her anymore because her husband was jealous, "which was not a problem before." We used to be excellent friends at high school. After another six months, she talked to me again for about a week until she said, "By the way, I have your money, and I'm going to pay you now, but I wanted to ask you. Can you lend me 500 dollars more and I'll pay you everything by the end of the month? I told her I could not borrow that money now, but thank you for contacting me. Two days later, she blocked me from Facebook and my cell phone, so I could not talk to her.

In conclusion, if I kept my mouth shut about how much money I was making and about my job, there is a good chance that I would still have a friend and the money.

In A Relationship 1

"Silence is a true friend who never betrays" -Confucius.

I used to hang out with my friends all the time; the idea of having a girlfriend in middle school was just an idea.

My town was small, and we didn't have a middle school. I had to go to a different town for middle school, which sometimes was one and a half hours walking if nobody gave me a ride there. Generally, in the morning, somebody would give me a ride to school, so I just had to walk back home, which was not a big deal because I had more friends who also did that, and we walked together.

In middle school, my friends were usually two years older than me. This friend wanted to introduce me to a beautiful girl, but I was terrified, thinking I had to talk to her. This girl, whom I will call Yina, was beautiful. She had a beautiful smile, her eyes were brown, and her skin was golden brown. Every time she sees me, she smiles and raises one eyebrow, paralyzing me; I cannot move or say anything. My friend told me that she wanted to date me, and I immediately said no; there was no way. I always invented some excuse not to meet her in person because I was afraid to do that, but I didn't want my friends to know that because they would take advantage of that to bully me.

Yina had a problem: she didn't know how to keep her mouth shut, and every time she met someone, she told her friends, "Oh, I kissed that guy. Oh, this guy invited me to a restaurant, and we kissed after that. She didn't know that she had a terrible reputation because of all the talking she did. She thought her friends would be happy for her, but it was the opposite. Everyone who met her knew she was straightforward and didn't see her for her beauty. Everyone just wanted to have a good time whit her expecting to kiss her or grab her butt because of the reputation she built herself.

I liked Yina, but she was on a different level than me, so I couldn't talk to her ever because I was too scared. No one took her seriously because she hadn't learned how to keep her mouth shut.

In A Relationship 2

We should keep our relationships as quiet as possible for many reasons. We can lose relationships that have yet to start.

In 2006, I started high school in a bigger town than mine. I was very excited because all I could see at school were new faces, which meant new opportunities to make new friends. The high school I attended was small, but there were many students because it was very new; I was the 3rd generation at this high school. Many students were older than me because they did not have the chance to go to high school until this one opened close to their homes.

I met an excellent friend at school, and we always discuss relationships with girls. I was so excited to hear other friends' stories about girls that I had to make up some stories that never happened when they asked me; I made these stories so I could be part of these conversations. Sometimes, the stories I told were true, but not for me. Sometimes, I heard others talk about this, and I made them my stories to tell, or sometimes, it was just a friend who said to me that and used it for me to be popular with other friends.

There was this guy who was very popular with women. I'll call him Mike. Mike always told the best stories. Every week, Mike came up with new experiences, and it was exciting for me to listen to him because he had the most knowledge from all the other friends there. In my second year of high school, I thought a girl was beautiful, but I was scared to talk to her, so one day, I asked Mike. Hey Mike, I like a girl; she doesn't have a boyfriend, but I want to ask her if she wants to hang out with me; how can I make her interested? What should I tell her or ask her for that? Mike was curious because this was the first time I had asked him a favor like this. He wondered which girl was the one that I was talking about, so from a distance, I pointed at the girl; he looked at her and, after about 30 seconds, Mike told me this: the best way to approach someone is to give her a gift first, like candy or chocolate, and then ask for a date after that. That's it? I responded, yes, he said, that's it, but I'll tell you what, that woman is too skinny for you; you might need somebody else. I thought Mike was right because he was the expert, so I thought of taking more time to ask her. After two weeks, I was surprised that Mike was dating this girl. I was in shock. I was thinking, hey!!! Mike told me she was too skinny, so why is he dating her now? It seems he likes her, and she likes him because their relationship lasted even after we finished high school.

This might be a different story if I keep my mouth shut with Mike; I think it's better not to tell others what we plan to do because they can take our idea and make it theirs.

In A Relationship 3

I believe it gets harder and harder to have a relationship; the longer we wait, the harder it is.

I have friends who have had a girlfriend since they were 13 or 14. It was not until I was 18 that I had my first girlfriend. She was beautiful, and I wanted to make her happy in all possible ways. I told her that I would make her happy forever and that she was my first girlfriend, and she couldn't believe it.

I was very excited and always talked about her with my friends and family. I told everybody that I would marry my girlfriend and that she was perfect. Not everyone agreed, and some of my friends were trying to sabotage our relationship for some reason. Since it was my first girlfriend, I didn't know how to treat her, so I tried to be the best boyfriend ever. I send her a love text before bed and a good morning text when I wake up. I long texted love every time we had one more month, and I promised her a happy life. We planned the names of our kids and dogs and the color of the curtains our windows would have. I should keep my f mouth shut because not everyone was happy to see that I was happy; even my best friends were not satisfied that I was always pleased and talking about her. Nobody gave me good advice, and they tried to show me that I was living in a fantasy, that a happy life does not exist in a relationship, but I was happy, and I was sure that I wanted her in my life.

Well, a few years later, we broke up, and it was excruciating for me because all the talking and the promises I made were nothing anymore. It would be better to enjoy the moment and keep the relationship between two people. It would be better to keep my mouth shut and not make any promises anymore. "Action talks more than words."

If you want to show somebody you care about that person, don't promise anything; instead, keep your mouth shut and do something for that person. Show appreciation with actions, not words.

In A Relationship 4

Why do we post on Facebook and other social media that we are in a relationship? I'm sure there can be many different answers, but the most common is to let our friends and family know that we are now with someone. Let me tell you something: nobody gives a s#!t that you are in a relationship. We do this to show the other person that we care about our relationship, and we want others to know about it; we think this will make our partner happy, but most of the time, it is uncomfortable because then other people will go to see the person and will start judging about how they look if they got money if they are popular, if they travel or not if they went to school or not and some many more reasons. A relationship should be between the interested persons only, and believe me, it will be much better that way.

After I suffered from my first relationship, of course, I had it on Facebook so the person would know that I cared about her; I was not particularly eager to put my relationships on Facebook anymore. One day, my girlfriend told me I should put our relationship on Facebook, and I asked her why. She said to me so everyone knows that you are taken, and I told her that it doesn't work that way, but she insisted. I posted that I was in a relationship, and many friends were reacting: oh wow, congratulations, it was about time; you got this tiger; these were some comments I received. I knew most of these comments were fake, and the reality was different; I knew some people would go right away to see what type of girlfriend I had. For her, it was different; she received comments like hey, how could you date a guy like him? This will not work; do you know what type of guy he is? And some comments from guys like how could you do this to me? Let's hang out anyway; I'm second in the line; I'll be here for you when he is gone; this guy has another girlfriend; dump him; he is not suitable for you; even one of my friends tried to date her. She said Hey, do you know Edgar I said yes, he is an excellent friend, then she said Well, he is inviting me to the movie theater, just me and him. I told him I was with you, and he said it was okay. Your boyfriend also hangs out with other girls so that you can do the same thing.

93% of our comments were about why we were not suitable for each other, and the remaining pretended to be happy about that. I'm sure they didn't give a s#!t for that. So, one more time, I learned that we must keep our f mouths shut.

In A Relationship 5

Let's talk about marriage. This should be the most significant commitment we make. Let me ask you something: Should we tell our spouse everything and anything we do? Sometimes, it works, but sometimes, it is better to keep our mouths shut.

My friend Luis is a great man; we have been friends since elementary school. I first met him when I was five, and he was 2. Our first meeting was not the greatest because he decided to throw some objects at me the first time he saw me. Well, one of these objects was a dog made of porcelain. Well, it went right to my head, and it broke, and I was bleeding. My first reaction was to punch him, but hey, he was only two years old. He didn't do it on purpose. I didn't do anything to him.

Twelve years later, I started working with his dad and uncle in Mexico; they have a big flower company. Luis was in charge of some significant responsibilities that required talent and skills, and he always did the job well, so I wondered if he threw that dog on purpose 12 years ago.

At first, when I saw him working, he did it with passion, and I thought that he had some talent to do work; he is dedicated and creative, always wants the best result, and he studies the situation to make sure the best result will come out from it. Luis always talked about new ideas, how to make more money and everything he would do to improve the company. When he was in college, he got married, and his mind changed slightly, but he still focused on the main ideas he had before. I wanted to do business with him because I thought he could be a great business partner. When I came to the United States and started working and saving money, he gave me some business ideas. Hey, Geo, he told me. I have been thinking about what is needed around this area, and I found that too many parties are going on and there are not enough tables to meet the demand; why don't we put a table and chair rental business? I think there is a significant demand for it. It could be a great extra income; would you like to invest in a company like that?

I didn't want to sound too excited, but this was the opportunity I was waiting to have some business with him. I asked him how many tables and chairs we should start with, and he replied, " I think if we start with 30 tables and 300 chairs, it will be perfect, " I told him I'd send you the money, and you do the rest. As I was expecting, he did a great job; he presented a business idea with so many good details that if I presented this idea to Bill Gates, he would buy tables and chairs for the entire state of Mexico.

It was great, and we did a few more business after that, and all of them were good. We went on a trip to Colombia and saw ample business opportunities together. I was very excited to create this business idea with him, and we spent hours and hours putting the details together. It was exciting just thinking of making this idea come true. We planned the details, and when he returned to Mexico, he told me he had told his wife the idea and all the details and what she had thought about it. She thought this was ridiculous and there was no way to make this happen. We were crazy and probably did some drugs in Colombia that made our minds fly too much. Luis tried to convince his wife that this was a good idea and explained that this was on a different level; it didn't go well. She did not understand, and I told Luis.

Luis, this is going to happen a lot. You are excited, and you want to share this excitement with your wife instead of getting support and getting the same excitement you are expecting; sometimes, you will get a rejection and bad vibes that will make you feel down about the idea. I think it is better to keep your f mouth shut about any idea you have until this idea comes true because otherwise, this could ruin the plans and make you feel miserable and incompetent, so let's keep our mouths shut until we make this come true about that. He agreed with me, and until today, in 2023, we are still planning how to make this business idea come true, but now it is just between him and me.

My conclusion from this experience is that no matter who you are with, they might not share the same excitement that you do, so you have to analyze carefully and see if what you are about to share with someone is going to be good for you or if it's better to keep your f mouth shut until you get the results.

In A Relationship 6

My previous experiences taught me that keeping relationships secret is a lot better. It's not a secret from everyone, but keep it private, especially from social media. Unless you want attention and recognition from others, I think there is no need to inform the world what is happening in your romantic life.

I have kept my relationship private from social media and others because others don't like it when you are happy. People typically ask Hey Geo, what happened with your girlfriend? I thought you were going to marry her; at the beginning of my relationship, I told everyone yes, I was still with her, and we were still together. I was delighted to share that I had a beautiful girlfriend until almost everyone was saying. You know what? I don't think that will work; your girlfriend is from another country and never works. Geo, I heard your girlfriend works in another country; relationships never work from afar. You have to get out of that relationship; she is not for you, and I can tell that from far away. All these "good vibes and advice people gave me about my girlfriend and how and why this will never work made me wonder if it was better not to share more details with all of them. That is what I did, and now that people know I'm single and have nobody with me, they seem happier when they ask, hey Geo, where is your girlfriend? I just replied you know what? You were right; a relationship doesn't work from a distance. You were right, so I'm single now; then they replied, you see, I told you, I knew it is better to stay single, but don't worry, most of these people who said being single is significant is because they are married or in a relationship.

So, one more time, keep your f mouth shut about your relationship. I talk to my girlfriend very often; she is in another country; we have been together for some years, and every time I go to see her or she comes to visit me, it is lovely; we have a great time together when we keep our relationship between me and her.

You, my dear reader, try this for yourself. If you have families, friends, or coworkers who always try to advise you that your relationship is not going anywhere, try this: next time they ask you, hey, how is your relationship going? Tell them no more relationships for now. You were right all this time, and thank you so much for telling me that; you know what? I'm going to start to listen to your advice more often. You are wise, and I'm lucky to be close to you. Dear reader, try this, and you might be surprised by all the stress and pressure you get off your shoulders.

At the Gym 1

"Work hard in silence; let your success make the noise."

How often have you said I will start going to the gym the following Monday, and that Monday never came? You have to respect yourself more and start doing what you said you would do. Keep focusing on yourself and forget about looking good in front of others. Don't try to impress somebody who doesn't even like or care about you.

This is a book of action. The action is that you have to be like a horse in a race. You cannot watch what others are doing and be intimidated by them because they have more discipline than you. Just keep your mouth shut and start going to the gym already.

As a kid, I watched many action movies with my family. This movie was an inspiration for me to start working out. Movies where the actors were: Jean-Claude van Damme in Blood Sport, Arnold Schwarzenegger in Commando, Sylvester Stallone in Rocky Balboa, Tony Jaa in Ong-Bak, Scott Adkins in Boyka and of course Bruce Lee in Enter the Dragon. All this movie inspired me to move my body, jump, run, climb trees, and jump from the roof. Jumping out the roof was not always the best idea, but when flying, I felt like I could do anything and reach any goal. This was the best sensation I felt, and I was enjoying every second because kids don't want to impress their friends or put dates to start doing what they said they would do, but when we grow up, most of us forget that sensation of everything is possible. You don't have to wait until Monday to start doing what you know will make you happy; on this occasion, training like a movie starts to be one of them.

At the GYM 2

When I first started to work out, it was in kindergarten. We might not see it like that, but the truth is that when we jump, run, and play on the slide, we are moving our bodies, and all that excitement gives us more energy to do it repeatedly.

In elementary school, my favorite course was sports, maybe because we could play and go outside the classroom. In 3rd grade, my sports professor was excited when we talked about sports; we ran and played basketball, volleyball, and soccer. My professor, Roman, was very strict with us when we had to do some sports; he didn't like to play around and sometimes made the sports look hard. He classified our score per group. First, he took 100 meters of time and grabbed the best 15 from the first try. Then, he dedicated the rest of the time, approximately 1 hour and 15 minutes, to talking with this group; these were his words. The whole group came here. The first 15 people who got to the 100 meters first will be with me, and we will have fun together. The rest of the class can play whatever they want. I was in the 15-person group and excited to have more fun, but my smile disappeared immediately when he started talking. Ok, you guys think that you know how to run, but the truth is that if I put a turtle against you, there is a high chance that you will lose. They laughed at his words, and I was the first to talk. I said no; I think I can run faster than a turtle. The rest of the group also laughed. Well, this was my first contact with this professor; as you can see, it was not the best start for a kid who enjoys sports to open my mouth without thinking about what could happen if I made someone feel embarrassed in front of others. What is your name? The professor told me; my name is Geo, I answered, ok, Geovanny, let's see if you can run faster than a turtle after you run six laps around the entire field. I ran alone while the other guys were having fun with the professor. He was teaching them how to stretch correctly, warm up before each run, and breathe when we ran, and I was not part of that group just because, even as a kid, I didn't know how to keep my mouth shut.

Professor Roman, never repeat that class. Even though I was in the 15-person group, I never learned how to stretch correctly, warm up, and breathe when running. I felt like everyone was ahead of me, and I was trying to copy their moves, but it seemed that it was not that efficient. I got in 3rd place the first time we ran the 100 meters, but after two weeks, I was in 6th place. I don't know if that day was affected by my mouth telling the professor, but this could probably be a chance because the first time we ran, I was very excited, and I thought I could get first place if I trained more. That year, we competed at the state level, and there were 24 schools; we got 4th place, but it wasn't me who represented our school that made me feel that I was not good at running, so I didn't join the team the following year.

Dear reader, as you can see, there is no age where keeping your mouth shut can help you and maybe change the course of your life; some opportunities are gone because we don't know how to stay quiet in places we should. Especially when we try to look smart in front of others and put ourselves in embarrassing situations with someone else; this could cost a lot in the future. That professor seemed to not care too much about me after I made him feel dumb, and he didn't teach me what he had taught the other classmates.

At the GYM 3

One of my favorite seasons is Christmas, and I'm saying one of my favorites because my favorite season is EL DIA DE LOS MUERTOS. The same day in the United States is Halloween. We get together in Día de los Muertos, but Mexico differs slightly from the United States. Mexico has two days for trick-or-treating: one for the children and one for the adults. For the children, they make a Calabria with some pumpkin that is called chilacayote. The chilacayote is green, and when you open your hand and take everything from inside to clean and make eyes and smile, your hands turn dark. There is some pain that I cannot explain that pain is unique but is worth the result; then you meet with your friend to go for a treat or trick, usually with a group of 5 or 7 kids, and when you start receiving money, candies, and fruit is the best sensation. At the end of the journey, you divide everything equally and go home to show your parents what you get for the whole night. For the adults, it is different; they only have one group per town. My town usually had a group of 25 to 30 people, but this was also a lot of fun. We collected the candies, and usually, the families left a bag full of stuff between fruit, candies, money, and sometimes even beer or pulque. The fruit is sometimes raw, and there is a rule: in the dark, you can throw the raw fruit to others as long as it is raw and is not good to eat; that is some adrenaline and is fun to see when someone is next to you receive this in their bodies but is not fun when you are the one who received it, and others laugh about you.

Christmas is great to spend time with family and discuss what you have been doing during the year. But let's talk about what comes after that; let's talk about December 31st, the 12 goals we write on a piece of paper that we want to complete during the year. One of the most famous goals is to lose weight and to start going to the gym. In January, the gyms make more money because that is when most people get their membership gym, and usually, this lasts between one and two months when the gyms are packed. After that, it is just like the usual routine; many people have a gym membership, and it can last six months or even more without going a single day to the gym. I was doing this myself.

Now, many people put something on Facebook and social media like starting fresh, getting a gym rat on board, achieving goal #1, and changing my life to a fitness life. They usually take a picture in the gym to get compliments. They take pictures every time they go to the gym to get more compliments, but let me tell you what, people don't care about what you are doing or what goals you have. I'm not saying that putting pictures in the gym is terrible; I'm saying that don't try to impress others and focus more on yourself, don't let others know that you want to change, and unless these pictures are for your inspiration or to inspire others then do it, but this is just a piece of humble advice from someone that was doing all these things. Still, I was tired of people not responding how I wanted. It's better to keep our f mouths shut and start doing what is best for us. I like anime, and my favorite anime is Dragon Ball Z; it was when I saw a meme about Goku, I stopped posting pictures in the gym; the meme was something like this. "Goku was training on another planet with Kaiosama for 158 days, training every day without posting any pictures. You cannot get 10 minutes in the gym without letting everyone know you just got there, but nobody cares." Then I thought, you know, that is right. I should train without posting any pictures. I should keep my mouth shut and start working on getting better.

My dear reader, if you want to change and start doing what is best for you, please, I am begging you to get your ass up and go to the gym; no more pictures there unless that motivated you to keep going; otherwise, keep your f mouth shut and do what you said you were going to do.

AT THE GYM 4

We talked about one of the most famous goals for the new year: lose some weight, start going to the gym, eat more healthily, but what comes after that? Let's talk about what comes after three weeks of the new year; many pictures are not on Facebook anymore, and many friends have disappeared from the gym. Why don't we see photos and stories on social media anymore? I think we all have some friends who start very motivated, and we see some regular pictures showing that they are serious about changing lives. We don't know the motivation pictures anymore, and we think they just decided to stop posting and focus more on making and working, but the truth is different: they lost motivation and decided to take a day break. Next week sounds better, but after that, they didn't see any results anyway; it is not worth the time and money because they didn't see any change in 2 or 3 weeks.

To be clear, I am not judging anyone here because I was like that; I am trying to get the idea that it is very easy to talk, open our mouths, and show off that we are ready to change, prepared to take the step. We speak and post on social media to get that attention, get likes, and get other people's time to comment something positive, but once we get satisfied and lose that motivation, oh, surprise, the real battle starts right there. That is when we have to show if we have what we need to keep going to improve our lives. It took me six years of putting the same goal on the new year, "start going to the gym," to understand that we don't have to wait until next year to put that goal; we don't have to wait until next month to start doing what is best for our body, take some action today, set some goals today and make a plan to develop but start doing it today. Please don't show off anything; let the results speak for themselves. Keep your F Mouth Shut and start doing it, KEep YOur F MOuth SHut, And STart Doing IT; KEEP YOUR F MOUTH SHUT AND START DOING IT.

AT THE GYM 6

The gym is where many people go to stress out, forget about problems in real life, and pursue their fitness goals. Maintaining a considerate and focused environment is crucial; the last thing they want is someone interrupting that moment.

Respect for personal space:

Privacy during workouts. Most people don't like to get interrupted when they are trying to focus on a task that is sometimes difficult. Don't be disrespectful trying to break that concentration. If you want to talk with somebody, the gym is not an excellent spot; you can go to the mall on Sundays if that is what you want.

Now, let's talk about all those people who know precisely how you need to live your life. We all have some uncle, aunt, cousin, or familiar friend who tells us what to do because they for sure don't know how to keep their mouth shut; sometimes, the person who tells us how to live our life is not even our family member or friend; it might be just a random person who we might know because we live in the same city or neighborhood.

When I joined the military, the drill sergeants would always tell us what to do and if we made a little mistake, you have to be prepared for the next 5 minutes by doing push-ups or just standing up and listening to how the Sargent tell us that we were not good enough even you are doing the best you can. But that is part of the discipline we have to take to become a solider because, on the battlefield, one little mistake can cost your life or your battle bodies life's, which is a big deal for everybody to understand why it is essential to listen to others in the battlefield to get the best possible result. Well, yes, this is the military, and it is crucial to listen to our superiors to survive, but what about outside? What about listening to your uncle tell you what is best for you? Often, your money or your body, in this case, is good for you to work out or not.

One day, my nephew asked me what I recommended to him to lose weight and gain muscle. I told him what I learned in the military; I told him that we usually exercise without equipment, do some push-ups, squats for our legs and shoulders, run to do cardio, and so on. Axel was doing what I told him, and he was investigating other types of exercise for his body; while looking for more stuff, he found that the boxers do a lot of jumping. He asked me about that; hey uncle, what do you think about jumping the rope like the boxers do? Do you think this is a good idea he asks, well I'll be honest with you, I reply, I've never done that type of exercise in my life, but if the boxers do this type of work to gain condition, I think it is good to try it and see the results for yourself.

Axel was living with my aunt in the city because he was going to college in that city and wanted to look more athletic and presentable at his school; he was running and jumping the rope for about one week until he called me and asked me again, hey uncle can I ask you something, of course, I reply, well you know I'm living here with my aunt and her daughters which they are my aunts as well. Well, I have been working out and running as you suggested to me, plus I have been doing this extra exercise, jumping the rope for one week when Mary, the oldest daughter, came to me and told me that I should stop doing what I'm doing. She told me that jumping the rope is terrible for the waist and that if I didn't want to get hurt and possibly fraction, I should stop doing this immediately. Do you think I should stop doing this? Well, let me ask you some questions. How do you feel after working out? Axel: I feel good and have more energy. OK, has your aunt Mary ever practiced jumping the rope or has any experience jumping it? Axel: Nope, she never tried this because someone told her it is bad; I don't think she practices any exercise. Well, Axel, here is my advice and listen carefully, there are always people who are going to tell you what to do and what is best for you and what not, people that never had any experience especially are going to tell you what your idea is terrible and why you should stop doing it. Please don't listen to them; don't listen to people who only pay attention to you when you are about to change something to do better. These people never risked changing their lives, and they think it is impossible to do something because they give up on the first try or, even worse, they never tried because someone told them what is good and what is not. Listen to your heart and follow your dreams, read, educate yourself, and don't let people ruin your plans and inspiration to be better.

Dear reader, from my own experience, many people have told me what to do and what not to do; people who never dare to dream will try to make you give up on your dreams. Here is my advice: don't let anybody, no matter how close it is to you, don't let them ruin your dreams, work hard, and follow your dreams that will make you happy. You will find a lot of obstacles in the way, especially if you are following your dreams, but keep your mouth shut and focus on what is essential. Listen to all the advice, but take only the good ones and listen to your heart.

AT THE GYM 6.5

WHAT HAPPENS EVERY DAY IN LIFE?

If you are going to start going to the gym, keep your f mouth shut, don't post pictures on social media, and don't start posting pictures before and after a week of going to the gym in January. Nobody cares if you are beginning, have ten years, or have lost 6 pounds; nobody cares what is happening in your life; the good actions people don't care. Just start going to the gym without opening your mouth to communicate what you are doing. Strat, go, and repeat yourself in the mirror that you will be a better person than yesterday.

This can happen daily; there is always an excellent opportunity to shut your mouth. I remember when I booked a flight from Minneapolis to Mexico City. This was like one year after COVID-19, and the restrictions to travel are still going on; you have to show proof that you didn't have COVID-19 and are healthy enough to travel. Usually, this test has to be done 48 hours before travel, plus the card that you have the COVID-19 vaccine. Most clinics in Minnesota make this COVID test free for you. I was going to do the test at the clinic, and everything was ready; the personnel at the clinic were preparing everything for the test, and I was almost ready to enter when they called my name and told me what room. Then I stopped and opened my big mouth; I said, yes, I need this test to travel; what did you do? The nurse asked me, "Well, I'm doing this test to travel; that is a different procedure the nurse said. Then I asked, but the test was the same, right? Yes, the test is the same, but if it is for travel, you must pay 180 dollars.

My mouth again, I had to pay 180 dollars for the same test that was going to be done for free, and it took more time. I was lucky to receive it the same day because typically, for travel, you have to make an appointment, and I was going to fly in two days, so I had no time to make an appointment. Ultimately, I did the same test the same day but with 180 dollars of difference that I could have saved if I had kept my mouth shut when nobody asked me anything.

AT SCHOOL 1

"It is Better to Keep Your Mouth Closed and let People Think You are a Fool than to Open it and Remove all Doubt." -MARK TWAIN

Let's discuss one activity we must do almost daily during the most critical years of our lives: going to school. School is significant because it is where we learn and develop skills we will use for the rest of our lives. Also, we can find what we are passionate about to follow our dreams.

I started kindergarten in 1995, and it was a bad experience the first three weeks because every day, I had to leave home and go home with many strangers, so I cried every time I had to leave because I was scared. It didn't matter if the teacher picked me up at home. The result was always the same. This was true until I found what, 27 years later, I call my best friend, whose nickname is "El Chiles. "Chiles was the opposite of me; he didn't know how to stay quiet and liked to explore and learn new stuff daily. Chiles found me crying one day when I arrived at kindergarten and got close to me; what is the matter he asked, nothing, and go away I replied; he sat next to me and told me, come here, let's go outside. I'll teach you how to catch some crickets, and if you want, I'll eat one if you stop crying. I laughed after hearing what he would do to make me stop crying. Since then, I found the great feeling of making friends and exploring the world could be interesting. After that day, I wanted to be on time to go to kindergarten because Chiles taught me some interesting stuff, like catching crickets, playing on the slide, jumping the rope, and more.

Could a 4-year-old kid learn that sometimes keeping the mouth shut could be more beneficial than just saying what we think now? I don't know if we could because I remember Chiles and I were playing with paint one day. We started to put paint on the walls; after playtime, the professor asked who did this, and Chiles said I did. When I was going to say that I also did it, he looked at me and told me to shut up. The professor punished him and told him he would stay after class to organize everything. I felt terrible inside; I felt guilty, which was horrible. I wanted to puke, so I came to the teacher and told her that I was also painting the walls. She looked at me, smiled, and said OK, then you will also stay after class to organize everything. After that, I felt much better, and Chiles and I stayed after class and organized the tables and chairs the professor was helping. It was fun to do these activities, mainly because I put the chair of one girl I liked next to mine so we could sit together the next day.

Two things I learned from this experience. One, cleaning, organizing, and putting the trash in the trash cans should not be considered a punishment because we think cleaning our environment is a punishment instead of a virtue. Two: if we do something terrible, we have to confess because this will take some weight off our shoulders, and we will learn that if we do bad things, these things will have some consequences; so, in this case, I think it is better to say something instead of keeping our mouth shut even if someone else, or we think is better to stay quiet, if we do something terrible is better to accept that, and said that we did it.

AT SCHOOL 2

Dear reader, let's do one activity now. Strat to putting your name in the blank space.

I _____

Then, put something you remember it would've been better if you kept your mouth shut.

Remember when:

_____
_____
_____
_____
_____
_____
_____
_____
_____
_____
_____

Dear reader, you may remember more than one time that it would've been better if you kept your mouth shut, but don't worry, this is more common than you think; usually, we believe that we are the ones who have to do more challenges in life. We see social media and so many people happy putting their vacations and luxurious life that we think, wow, if that were me, it would be perfect; that is what I need to be happy. The truth is that everyone has different challenges in life, and everyone has problems; no matter if one is a millionaire person, they also wish they could have a simple life sometimes.

 This exercise you just did will help you remember that it could be better. We are not perfect and don't have an ideal life, but this is the beauty of life when we can get better than yesterday. The more challenges we conquer and the more people we help, the better we feel about ourselves. Do another exercise. When you get outside, take one coat that you haven't used for more than three months, walk by the streets, and when you see somebody who might need a coat, give it to that person. This gesture will make you feel great; helping someone without expecting anything in return is one of the most satisfying gifts that we can get to make us think that we are in this world for a reason.

This book is a book of action for everyone who wants to start doing what they always said they would do. To start that project that scared you the most, to go to the school that you will always want, or take that job that makes you happy, to start going to the gym, eating healthy, replacing some bad habits with good habits, well the opportunities to start fresh and do what makes you happy, the options are endless; this is your time now. From now on, we will do some exercises in every chapter, and remember to keep your mouth shut and start doing what is best for you without announcing that to the world. Let the results and your actions speak for you, which will be louder.

AT SCHOOL 3

I have not been that good at school since elementary school because I preferred to go outside and do more activities outside the classroom. I always depended on my classmates to do homework. Eventually, someone was always willing to teach me how to do the homework or the activities I lost because I was not in the classroom when the professor was teaching them. This was my modus operandum during school. In the tests, I usually studied one or two nights before the tests, and I was passing the classes, so I was happy with that.

I was first generation in middle school and 3rd generation in high school; lucky for me, there was no entry test in middle school because I did not know almost anything then. Whenever we had to do activities in a group in middle school, I was always in the group with my friend Sandra. Sandra was doing almost everything for me, and when we had to present in class, she told me, Hey Geo, here is your part; you have to talk about this in class, memorize what I wrote in this paper, and present this when is your time, then you will be fine. Sometimes, that was easy if it was some topic that I liked or knew before, but sometimes the topic was complicated, and when it was my turn, I was shaking, and I couldn't say the words correctly even though I was reading what Sandra wrote in the notes for me. My friends were laughing at me, which made me more nervous, so every time I had to present, it was the worst moment for me. Typically, it was two or three minutes of talking, but it felt like hours that I had to speak in front of the whole class. Dear reader, I don't know if you ever felt that sensation in the class, that pressure that makes your voice go away and shake you when you have to present something. For some people, this is a natural talent; they get in front of people, and they can talk for hours naturally, but for some others, like was my case, we panic and feel like that is something that we should be able to avoid or not participate at all if you don't want to. We don't have a choice regarding school; we all have to do this at some point. Even if we don't want to or feel like this is the worst that can happen to us, we still have to do it.

During high school, I felt like I had everything under control because, for some reason, I passed the test we had to do to get accepted. I always thought it would be like someone else would be there for me every time I needed it. I was at the parties, and every time I could, I skipped classes and went outside to hang out with my friends. We usually do this on Fridays to live the life we call it. There was this friend, Areli, she was in the top 10 students all the time. I have invited her many times, and this is my advice. Areli, let's go party. Don't do too hard; you have to enjoy high school while you can because you will regret it, and it will be too late when that happens. No matter what I said to her, I couldn't convince her that I was doing the right thing to enjoy life, and she was wrong because she was always studying and being in the top 10 students. I laughed at her many times and liked to share my adventures with her, so she felt bad because she was not enjoying herself like I was. For college, you have to take an entry test and pass it to get accepted; before we did the test in different schools, maybe two months before graduating high school, I came one more time to Areli, and I told her to her face. Areli, tell me, what is the difference between you and me? You are among the top 10 students with no adventures and good memories, more than just being pressured constantly. Maybe you are stressed about all that studying you have to do. I am here with all these adventures and good memories to remember for the rest of my life, and guess what? We both are going to graduate at the same time. You have better notes than me, but that doesn't matter; all your effort does not matter now. She kept quiet. It seems like she was thinking that maybe I was correct, perhaps I was right, and she wasted the best years of her life. We did the test to go to college, and we got the results three weeks later; when the results came, she came to me and said, hey, geo, which college are you going to? What career do you want to chase? I looked at her and told her, Areli, I didn't pass the test, I didn't get accepted to college, I don't know what I'm going to do.

She looked at me, and it seemed like she knew before me that I didn't pass, and she put on a big smile like something that you had been working for years finally got worth it; honestly, I don't know if she was that happy because she gets accepted or because I didn't, but I think it was the second one. She looked at me like she had been waiting long to tell me this. I'll answer your question now; this is the difference between you and me: I'll go to college, and you won't; I'll be a professional, and you won't; I'll make my dreams come true, and you won't. You see, all this hard work pays off; you are an idiot that is going to work in the agriculture side because that doesn't require a college degree, not even a high school degree; you should have given up sooner, what you saw is what you reap, and you didn't sow any shit she told me. I couldn't reply because I felt like she wanted to cry, but she wanted to cry. I hurt her because I didn't know how to keep my f mouth shut, but she did it for me; she shut me up nicely. At that moment, I understood that words can hurt badly. I hurt her even though that was not my intention, and she hurt me back. She hurt me badly with the words that she said to me, and I was wondering if that is how she felt when I told her all that stuff. I was happy for her that she passed, and I was pleased because she proved me wrong; she proved to me that hard work always pays off.

She was like an awakening for me because I promised myself I'd think carefully before I opened my big mouth in the future. Also, she inspired me. She proved to me I was wrong. I also wanted to prove to her that she was wrong about me. I don't think I'd be that motivated to get a college degree in construction if it wasn't for her. Her words hurt me, but they also woke me up. I never apologized to her, but I hope she read this. Areli, I'm so sorry because I did not know how to shut my mouth with you. Thank you for teaching me that lesson that day.

AT SCHOOL 4

After I didn't pass the college entry test, I didn't know what to do next. I found a job in my town in agriculture, as Areli was saying; at first, I was scared, but then I realized that it was good to learn something new, especially in one of the most critical areas: agriculture. I found very nice people there who were willing to teach me how to grow vegetables and flowers. It was ok, but I couldn't stop thinking about Areli's words and wondered if she was right about me.

After one year, I went to my aunt's house in the cities to try the test again; in the meantime, my friends from high school were telling me to switch careers; instead of doing civil engineering, they wanted me to do something more manageable, something that doesn't requires ability in math and science, they told me to do accounting or electronic engineer because the college they went needed more students and 95 percent of the students who present exam pass. I was sure what I wanted to do, so I told my friends I would stay with civil engineering; after I got the results, I found out I didn't pass again. I felt depressed, and I didn't want to wait for another year, but I had no choice because that was the closest public school that offered this career; I waited another year and did the test again. This was my 3rd time doing it. Something happened to me before I took the test for the 3rd time.

First, at my work, during the waiting time, I was excited to share my dream with my supervisors. I thought that they would be happy for me to keep trying after the second fail. Well, I went and talked to them about my dreams. One day, I want to build roads and buildings, infrastructures, and do all kinds of construction; my dream is to be a civil engineer; well, one of them just laughed at me; the engineer is not for idiots, he said you are an idiot, don't waste more time and just realize that you are going to work for us for a long, long time, this was almost something that Areli told me nearly three years before. The other laughed at me, but he told me it was worth dreaming. My aunt, on the other hand, was mad at me. Don't make your mom spend more money on that ridiculous idea of you becoming an engineer. This is going to be your third time, and I'm sure you are not going to pass again; accept it is you born poor, you are going to die poor. It was so sad that I heard from the people I work with and my family that I was good for nothing. Dear reader, if you are going to school, planning to go to school, or dream about becoming a professional, give yourself a favor and save some disappointments, and you know what to do. Keep your mouth shut, keep your dreams to yourself, and talk to the people who can help you achieve your goals. One more thing: Keep dreaming. I am a civil engineer who has now built some roads with a big company, and guess what? All the people who told me I wouldn't do it are the first people who now told me I always believed in you. That's why "DON'T BEAR IN MIND THE FLATTERIES OR THE OFFENSES" unless the offenses are to improve yourself.

Your Next Move 1

"Half of Seems Clever is Keeping Your Mouth Shut at the Right Times."

It's natural for everyone to make plans when they haven't even started college or moved to a different city or job; there is something like the next move. In boxing, your opponent mustn't know your next move. Playing chess is crucial; if your opponent doesn't know your next move, that is how the chess strategy works. Be good at hiding what your next move is going to be.

In college, I needed a car to move around the city. I was looking on Facebook marketing and Craigslist, and finally, I found this Honda CRV 2002; I bought the SUV for 2000 dollars and thought it was an excellent deal. Then I wanted to modify the SUV a bit, then put some money into tires, and I was looking for a superb sound system. Finally, I found a place to buy a good amplifier and bought two 12's comp kickers. I needed a big wire, but they were expensive, and the installation was even more costly. I decided to buy the amplifiers and the suitable cables and install everything myself; in the end, I put more speakers in 4 doors and added an extra two outside that I mounted in the 12's kickers.

I spent 2200 dollars on the sound system, more than the SUV when I finished everything. I told my dad, and he was mad at me; he said it was a waste of money. He would never make such a mistake as buying a sound system for a car, which made me feel bad, and I decided to speak with my supervisor at work. I thought he would make me feel better, but he did not. He told me that if he were me, he would take the wire cutters and cut all the wires and through everything in the trash; that made me feel bad, but when I was inside the Honda, and I put on music, I like to turn the volume up, that satisfies me. I felt that I should not tell others what my plan was for the future because not everyone would feel the same joy and excitement that I felt.

Dear reader, for this chapter, let's do this activity. Right down something that you bought those others think is a bad idea but makes you feel good. It could be a sound system or a tattoo; in the blank space, draw a picture of yourself enjoying what you bought that makes you happy. This will remind you that sometimes people will not share your ideas, but you have to do it because it will make you feel happy, which matters.

Your Next Move 2

Another time we should keep our mouths shut is if we will make our next move to make money. When Ratiman came to my town and hired me, he was good because he knew how to do business; he and his brothers bought 3 acres of land very cheap in my city because the owner was urgent to sell. He also was known for using his resources in the best way possible; some men's trash is another man's treasure, he used to say. I was delighted that I was working with him because I wanted to learn how to use my resources best.

Ratiman has a lot of great ideas all the time. One day we were cutting flowers, but the prices were meager; I thought right away, damn, that is too bad that the prices are low right now because there are a lot of flowers, and now all of this is going to trash. Raiman was smiling, and I wondered how he handled that; if we cut the flowers to trash them, how could he still smile for that? If I were him, I would probably be crying and complaining because the prices were low, so I asked him, hey Ratiman, how can you still smile in situations like this? You are losing money and still smiling. Tell me why. He looked me in the eyes and said, Geo, this is an excellent opportunity to return to the soil some organic material that we take from the soil; if you want your soil to produce a good product, you also have to return something to it, most of the peoples here want to take everything without putting back something, and then after some years they are wondering why the soil is not that good anymore, why the product doesn't have that same quality like a few years ago. Well, here is the answer. All the trash you see, if you call it trash, I call it golden dust. It is golden dust because, with the chopper machine, I will turn this flower into dust. Then I'm going to return this to the soil so it has something to absorb, and all this is organic material, which is a golden dust for the soil. I was speechless about what I was watching and hearing. That was the first time that I saw that someone's trash was another's treasure, but now I was living that, and I was fascinated.

I wanted to learn more from Ratiman. I liked working for him; he was expanding and wanted more land to grow more flowers. I saw an opportunity here, so I asked him hey, how big is the land that you are looking to buy, he said about the same size as this one, maybe three or more acres, and how much are you willing to pay for a good land, well if it has easy access to water, I am ready to pay 30,000 dollars for it. I was looking for something, and I found it. My uncle, who lived 20 minutes from my town, was selling land. I went and looked at the land, and it was perfect; it had easy access to water and was 3.3 acres. I asked him the price, and he said he wanted 15,000 dollars for the land. I was excited when I heard that; my uncle even told me to find someone to buy the land, and I could make some money on it if I could sell it more expensive without him knowing that I already had a potential buyer for that land. I talked to ratiman and said Hey ratiman if I found you a land that is cheaper than 30,000 dollar and is more than 3 acres would you buy it, and do you think that is fair if I keep some of that money to myself for the job I am doing he told me to explain myself, well I found a land that is cheap and is in good location., one day I was reading to a win, win deal well everyone wins in the deal so I explain to ratiman, the land is selling for 15,000 dollars you are willing to pay 30,000 dollar about you pay 25,000 dollars, I spend my uncle 20,000 dollar and I keep myself 5,000 dollars in the case everyone wins 5,000 dollars, he liked the idea and we went to check the land then he said yes I am going to buy it for 25,000 dollars, my uncle was not there when ratiman and I was checking the land but later on I when to see him and said hey uncle I found a buyer for your land, you are asking 15,000 and I am going to buy it for 20,000 the buyer is going to pay 25,000 and I will keep 5,000 for myself, when can we start the paperwork ? he stopped me and said hold on, hold on, hold on, why are you keeping 5,000 for my land, don't you heard what I told uncle I sold your land for 5,000 dollars more than you are asking for isn't this great? Well, nephew, he continues, those 5,000 dollars is a lot of money for you to keep; bring me that buyer, and I'll give you 200 dollars for yourself. I was in shock. I couldn't believe what he said; he only cared about the money I would get, not the extra money he would get. I went and talked to Ratiman and explained to him, and he just told me Well, this is an outstanding lesson for you to learn; you just lost 5,000 dollars because you should keep your mouth shut until the deal is done; then you can talk about it, but don't worry I am not going to buy that land I am going to keep looking for something closer.

Two things I learned from this, and you, my dear reader, I hope you can take advantage of this also: keep your f mouth shut if you are going to make a deal, don't talk to anybody about the benefit you are going to get for you work, even if is someone close to you, do the things quietly and your things will go better than you expect. Second, don't make any deal just by words; find some information about doing any business legally; in this case, make the seller sign some paper well they are signing to sell you for such an amount they cannot back up after you complete the deal and even if they are mad that you are selling for more, they cannot do anything about it, and I think it is a fair reward for your work so don't let anybody get in the middle of that.

Your Next Move 3

When you trust someone and care about them, don't lie to them because everything can start with a small lie, but then it can turn into a big lie and get worse when you have to involve more people so your lie can look true.

This happened to me when I was working in Mexico. My boss at that time was always very nice to me; he was strict but always wanted me to improve. He found me a job in the government; my job was to go to conferences and speeches to convince people to vote for the party working on getting reelected. We worked every two days to go to different towns, but when the elections happened, the party I was in lost the election, so the rest of the time, they moved me to pick up trash. When my boss, who found me the job, called me to check how things were going, I said Hi, everything is excellent here, well, that was my first lie, then everything would get worse from there. I call this:

"THE WEB OF LIES"

I once spun a tangled web of deception, ensnaring myself in half-truths and fabrications. It all began with a seemingly harmless lie to my boss—a lie that would ripple through my days like a stone cast into a still pond.

Picture this: I stood before him, the weight of my words heavy in the air. "I'm moving to a different city," I declared, avoiding his gaze. The truth? They had shuffled me into a role that involved little more than picking up trash. But admitting that felt like revealing a chink in my armor, so I chose evasion over honesty.

Curiosity flickered in his eyes. "Why leave town if the job is good?" he asked. A fair question—one that pricked my conscience. I conjured resolve and replied, "I've decided to relocate. Already secured a job elsewhere." His smile bloomed, and I basked in the warmth of his approval.

Yet the lie had taken root, and its tendrils crept deeper. He probed further: "What kind of work awaits you there?" Panic fluttered within me. "Public relations," I blurted. His enthusiasm swelled. "Fantastic! Best of luck," he said, unwittingly fertilizing my falsehood.

Days passed, and my boss's inquiries multiplied. "Show me pictures of your new city," he urged. "And your workplace." My palms grew clammy. The city existed only in my imagination, and my job was a phantom—a role I'd conjured to escape my trash-collecting fate.

Finally, I faced the mirror of truth. "Politics isn't my path," I confessed. "I quit." His disappointment etched lines on his face, but he extended an olive branch: my old job, waiting like a familiar refuge. I accepted, grateful yet burdened by the weight of my deceit.

Here's the lesson, etched into my soul: **Lies corrode trust**. They erode the foundation of relationships, leaving behind fragile scaffolding. So, dear reader, heed my missteps. When faced with choices, choose honesty. If you plan to move, say so. Avoid the snare of falsehoods that morph into monsters. For in the end, it's the truth that sets us free—the truth, unburdened by deceit's heavy chains.

And remember: **Trust gained is precious; trust lost is irretrievable.**

Your Next Move 4

One of my most significant moves was when I came to the United States, but of course, many people were questioning why, how, and when I would go here.

When I was working with Ratiman, they were bullying me because I couldn't get accepted into the civil engineering school in Mexico; then, one professor from the school that I didn't pass recognized me and told me, hey, this is your third time trying to enter this school, right? I was nervous, but I said yes, this is my third time trying; well, he responded there are just a few spots for the new students to get in; about 500 students do the test, and only 80 of them get accepted into this career that you want to get into. That made me feel better because I thought I was not so bad. Still, he said, there is a high chance that you do not get accepted again because an increased number of those 80 students get accepted because they know someone who can help them get in even if they don't pass that test. Sorry, but this is how the system works here. Don't worry. I'll tell you what to do. Take any engineering exam at any other university and do one semester there. Then, I can help you transfer to this university for this career. I was delighted to hear that because, finally, my dream would come true. I was very excited, so I told Ratiman and his brother, but they immediately laughed.

I didn't pass but did what the professor suggested and applied to electronic engineering at a different school. I got accepted. It was a highly complex class, and I was a little scared that I wouldn't pass the math class and the professor would not be able to help me. Everything was good, and my grades were okay for getting a transfer. Still, one month before I finished all the classes, my dad, who was in the US, came to Mexico and told me, Son, there is an opportunity that could change your whole life; your case gets accepted in the immigration center of the United States, and they want you to do an interview. Still, you only have three weeks to decide; this opportunity will disappear forever if you choose not to go. I was scared again because I needed to determine when, after waiting three years, it would finally be confirmed. I decided to take that opportunity and leave everything behind and start from Cero, but before that, I talked to some people in my town who were laughing at me because they knew how difficult it was to get that interview.

People were bulling me for the rest of the three weeks that I stayed in Mexico; they said things like, hey gringo when are you going to the USA and after that, they laughed at me so loud that it made me feel bad. People were wondering about that, and they tried to give bad advice or scared me, so I should not take that risk, but I noticed something: people are scared when we make some decisions that they are afraid to do or can't do. Just keep your mouth shut when some opportunity knocks on your door, and you will save a lot of stress and doubt about yourself.

Your Next Move 5

I thought that everything was going to be easy when I got to the United States, but I was wrong; the first thing I noticed here was that I was not going to start from zero; I was going to start from -1 because even if I want to order food, I need to speak English. I'm not too fond of mayonnaise, but it was hard for me to order a burger with no mayo; workers sometimes didn't understand what I was trying to order, so the burgers came with mayo because I didn't know how to say no mayo. That was only my first challenge; the second was finding a job because my dad told me that living in the USA was expensive and there were bills that I had to be responsible for every month.

I found a job picking up the trash at the mall because that job didn't require too much to speak. It was easy for me, although it was just part-time, but that was not enough to pay the bills, so I needed to find something else. I went to an office that helps people who don't speak good English find a full-time job. I saw something on the night shift from 11 pm to 7:30 am. That job was awful because I couldn't sleep during the day and had to stay awake all night, washing and disinfecting the machines that make the hot pockets. I didn't last more than two months in that job when I quit, but my dad was mad at me because I was building a bad reputation, and it would be harder for me to find a good job.

My dad took one day off to take me to the employee office again and left me there with my cousin who was living with us, knowing that I was quitting the jobs because I didn't like them. Still, I told my cousin I wanted to attend college here. I wanted to learn English at the school, well this was a bad idea because he told my dad what I was planning and my dad was a little bit mad because he knew how expensive it was to get to college here and he reader wanted me to work than thinking to go to college.

When my dad left me at the employee's office, the worker there told me why I didn't go to school; instead, I told him I had been looking for that since I came here. He mentioned that this job corps school across the United States is free, and they will teach me some trade and English if I need to. They would give me a GEG, the same as a high school diploma, plus a place to live and eat FOR FREE. This was unreliable. I found the best opportunity of my life, and I took it. I almost lost that opportunity because I was excited. I told my cousin what I was going to do, thinking that he was going to get excited. Instead, he told my dad that I was going to ruin my life and get in trouble with the government my whole life. He tried hard to convince my dad that it was a terrible idea to let me go to this school alone, but I think he was feeling bad because the apartment bills were only going to be between him and my dad. I was not going to put my part of the bills.

Luckily, my dad didn't try too hard to convince me to stay working, and I went to this school, which opened a new world of opportunities. That is one of the best risks I have taken so far.

Dear reader, if you are going to make a big move, please keep your f mouth shut because people might scare you or convince you that it is too much risk and you will ruin your whole life. Just take the risk if you think that can change your life for good, and if you listen to your heart, he will tell you that you should take the risk even if you are scared because that can be the door to a whole new world for you, full of excitements and adventures.

MAKING MONEY 1

"You Prove your Worth with your Actions, Not Your Mouth."

When I was a kid, I noticed something interesting about money. My mom always tried to hide the bills from us to count them, which made me more curious. I was always wondering what the purpose of that paper was and why mom hid them, but as a kid, you get more interested in the things people try to hide from you because I think it is our human nature to be curious about things and explore new stuff.

We are a big family, and I have a lot of uncles and aunts from my dad and my mom; sometimes these uncles give us money, but as a kid, you don't know what to do, or you might know that if you give this paper or coins in the store, they give you candies sodas and chips. If my uncle gave us a bill, my mom would always say not to show it to anybody because they would take it from me. Give it to me, and I'll save it for you instead.

At first, when I was getting older and comprehended more about money, I thought my mom shouldn't hide the money from us; instead, she should teach us how money works and let us have it as kids. But my mom just gave me good advice, maybe without her knowing, and that is to keep your mouth shut when making money because other people would like to share the money that didn't cost them anything.

Dear reader, this is the activity for this chapter. If you have money saved already, talk to someone you know who is successful in business or managing money and ask for their advice. Then, next month, you will apply what this person told you without telling anybody what you are working on. If you don't have any money, save 30 % of your monthly income, and then talk to the person you know who is good with money and ask them for advice about making money. So, write in this space.
I_____
__ promise to myself that I am going to follow the advice I got from _____ for the next three months. Maybe you think 30% of the income is too high, but dear reader, what you believe is what you can do; there are no limits, so don't get too short when discussing your benefits.

MAKING MONEY 2

When I was a kid, the only money I could get was the money I received from families, especially on Sundays after church, but it only lasted about 3 hours because I spent it fast. In 3rd grade, I found some way to make more money. It was playing with marbles, so I had to practice every day to be good at it, and I was an excellent player. Sundays after church, when about nine kids received their money, we got together and played with marbles, but we bet cash; there were different ways to make money; one we bet, and whoever lost gave the other the money, sometimes the marbles broke so the other way was to sell marbles, and when some kid didn't have more money, he could pay with marbles instead.

It was not until 9th grade when my cousin and I started working in agriculture. Still, it was only one day every two weeks, so it didn't count as a full-time job, and we didn't know how to work, but my uncle gave us a chance anyway to carry flowers from one place to another where we have to put flowers in the shadow so they don't die with the sun. My uncle pays us about 4 dollars for a working day of 8 hours, while a regular worker makes 8 dollars for about the same day. I didn't know if this rate was fair, but at least we could make some extra money to have fun.

One day, a guy from my town came to us and asked, " Hey guys, do you think you could help me this Saturday? I'm a little short of personnel, and some extra hands would greatly help me. We were happy to hear that because we usually had to look for work if we wanted to make extra money, but this time was different, so we immediately said yes, we could do that. We helped him for 8 hours, and when he paid us, we were surprised that he paid us 9 dollars, even more than what my uncle pays a regular worker who knew more than us. Plus, he gave us breakfast in the morning and water in the afternoon; we were speechless, but we just looked at each other, thinking that he might have made a mistake but we stayed quiet because we didn't want to correct him if he did make a mistake mistakenly, so we just said thank you for the pay and left immediately before he called us back to check how much he paid us. Three days passed, and we saw him coming to us again. We thought to run because he sure would tell us he had made a mistake, but he came and said, hey guys, our hearts were beating fast. Still, he asked us if we could help him again next Saturday. We replied with our heads because we couldn't say anything more, so he said OK, I'll see you guys then. Saturday came, and we were working, but he left us there alone, and my cousin and I were talking about, hey, do you think Mateo will pay us the same or not? Yes, my cousin responded, and he kept going. I don't know if he is stupid because we usually make 4 dollars for the same job. He is paying us 9 dollars plus giving us breakfast and a water break in the afternoon, well I reply I think he doesn't know how to pay people here, but let's not say anything so he can keep us paying this much then we were laughing because Mateo was stupid, we heard some voice coming from the tree next to us, hey guys would you like some fruit from this tree? Our hearts were beating even faster than before, so he came down the tree and gave us some fruit, and we just looked at each other and said nothing. We finished working, and then he paid us; our surprise was that he paid us the same amount as last time, but when we were about to leave, he said Hey, you guys, come here, tell me more about how stupid I am because I paid you more than the others guys around here, I heard you guys talking about me that I am silly for giving you breakfast in the morning and water break in the afternoon. Well, we almost cried in front of him. We couldn't say a single word. I felt so bad because I was talking trash about some excellent men who tried to help and inspire young kids to get a better future. He kept going: here is what is going to happen, guys. I will keep hiring you, but instead of 9 dollars, I'll pay you 5 dollars for one day of work. Do you agree with this? Yes, we replied, and that happened; next week, he only paid us 5 dollars.

This was very interesting because I think Mateo didn't care about the money he was giving us; he tried to teach us not to talk wrong about others, especially if you are working for them because this could have consequences. In this case, we lost almost half of our salary because we didn't know how to shut our mouths. I still feel bad because I broke the trust of a great man like Mateo. I think he is a good man, and I thank him for teaching us this lesson at a young age.

Dear reader, you don't have to make the same mistakes to learn; one of the purposes of this book is that you learn from other people's mistakes to make your life better, and you know that most of the time, it is better to keep our f mouths shut.

MAKING MONEY 3

If you are talking about making money, it is good to keep your mouth shut not just when you are making money but also when you are about to spend some money, for example, on the rent or bills you must pay.

After I graduated from college, I decided to take four months off because the pressure of school was too much, and I needed to forget about it. After the fourth month I took, it was time to find a job; in my college, having a career fair twice a year is widespread. I attended in March, and more than fifty companies were looking for engineers in construction. I applied and gave resumes to at least 12 of them. One was AMES Constructions for Renewable Sources, and I got accepted since I have some knowledge of solar panels plus an engineering degree; they were the first company to offer me a job, and I accepted. They paid well, and I was happy that my first company was a billion-dollar company. Since they paid me well, I didn't care too much about the rent then; I worked in Minnesota for about four months until one project opened up in Rapid City, SD.

I would move from Minnesota to South Dakota in the next few months and needed a place to live. I looked in many areas, but most of them required a contract for at least one year, and I was looking for something like a month-to-month contract because I wasn't sure how long I would live there. I found some guy who rented his house every year to a worker, but the contract was canceled for one year, so I talked to him, and this is what happened.

Me: I am unsure if I will keep working in the same state or if the company will relocate me to another one, so I am looking for a place to pay monthly.

The owner: Yeah, sure. Please tell me what you think, and perhaps we can modify the contract or do it monthly as you suggest.

Me: if we can make it monthly, I will take the place.

The owner: Yes, we can make it monthly, which is no problem.

Me: OK, and I can pay all the bills: gas, water, electricity, and internet. (Even though the owner told me that all the bills were already included)

The owner: If you can do that, that would be great.

Me: For example, if I pay for May and I get out on May 2nd, there is no need to refund any money, so you can find someone else to participate this month.

The owner: Yes, that would be helpful. I'll make sure I include that detail in the contract. Thank you for that suggestion.

That is how that conversation ended. A lot of people will think that it was a fair deal to offer that extra money. Still, the truth is that it was a mistake to open my mouth without thinking because if I am paying for a fair contract, there is no need for me to offer extra money when the owner already agreed to close the first deal without me having to pay the bills and other stuff. Ultimately, the owner was making more money, and I was spending some extra because I wanted to look friendly, kind, and responsible. I thought I was making a fair deal for both, but I fabricated this deal for myself, paying 30 % more than the first deal because I didn't keep my mouth shut.

MAKING MONEY 4

If you have a business and want to keep making good money, you have to keep your f mouth shut because there are people who cannot retain cash and want to share money that doesn't cost them anything.

One of my friends, Alex, told me something happened to him when he invested in a business that makes juice from natural fruits. The company was promised, and he decided to go for it.

It was around 2017 when everything started. I was checking social media and found something interesting: colorful juice made close to his town. But this wasn't normal because he had never known someone who made juice to sell in significant amounts around that area, so he looked, and it was the attractive logo; it was a strawberry with some ice and water that makes you drool just by looking at it. Then my friend went to check the page, and he noticed something; he saw his friend Ruben from high school was the one who managed the page, and more importantly, his friend was the one who made the juice.

Alex contacted Ruben; I told him how he was doing and asked if he wanted to talk in person. Ruben agreed, and they spoke, so he asked if he wanted to be a business partner. Alex knew some guy with money who was looking to invest in something. Ruben agreed, and they contacted Ernesto and asked for the plan together. Ernesto could help buy more equipment and put the product in many more stores, not just some restaurants where Ruben was already selling the juice.

After one year of investing, Ernesto considered moving the product to a different city. Still, Ruben and Alex had to move because they knew how to make the product. Ruben, who was married with two young kids, told Ernesto that he could move, but he would need support for his family when he was not going to work. Ernesto agreed to support him in the process for three months.

They became good friends but struggled to sell the product, for which Ernesto put all the money, and Alex and Ruben were just the logistics. Alex had some money saved, so Ernesto asked to put the investment plus support for Ruben's family. Ernesto had other investments, and someday, he was happy that he made good money in some of his other businesses, but then people wanted to see you well but not better than them. Ruben asked Alex if he could ask for more money from Ernesto because Ruben's family needed more to survive. Alex was mad because now Ruben was asking for more money, not just the amount they agreed to. They started to argue because the money was not enough now, and selling was not the best as Ernesto had promised.

In the business world, it is a risk. All the parties who are involved have to know that, in this case, the one who was investing more time and money was Ernesto, but once he brought up that other business that he had was producing good money, the problems started to happen, Ruben thought that Ernesto was focusing more in different business and wanted to make Ernesto looked terrible. Everything could be better if Ernesto hadn't shared his excitement with his partners, and the company perhaps would be big; that is why I think it is essential to keep your mouth shut if something is going well for you; not all people will share your excitement.

MAKING MONEY 5

If you win the lottery, the wise thing you can do right away is to keep your mouth shut for a long time until you decide the best way to use that money. What will happen if you tell your friends and family that you have a lot of money in your hands and that money does not cost you anything? People will start looking for ways to share that money with you. A family member will get sick, a friend's car will need some repairs, your uncle will need some extra cash to pay for rent, and your friend will come up with an enterprise idea that you can put your money into and is guaranteed success. But all these things will separate you from your money, and it will be challenging for you to get it back.

All people can make money, but most of the time, it is challenging to keep it. We are looking for ways to borrow more for a new phone that just came to the market, a plasma TV that now has more K in it and we have to get, or a car that we can afford if we make a monthly payment for six years.

Dear reader, money is crucial day to day. My advice for you, if you want to get more than you need, is to keep your mouth shut in every situation you can about money because that is one of the most common problems that we bring to our life if we tell people that we have some extra cash and we don't know how to use it. This will create envy from others, jealousy, and something we can put our lives at risk if people know that we have that money, so keep it quiet and learn new ways to invest that can produce good benefits for you and your family.

YOUR ACHIEVEMENTS 1

"Silence is one of the hardest arguments to refute."

Your achievements make you feel better because they are something that you consider fair rewards for your work. Not all people will agree with you on that, some people will think that you get lucky or someone else did the hard job for you like your parents or grandparents, but the truth is that it is nothing like that because if your parents or grandparents' inheritance you something if you don't know how to keep it or grow it you will lose everything.

For people, the word achievement can mean different things; for example, when you graduate high school, buy your first car, put your first business, or pass a math class. For me, it was to get accepted at the college, but it could also be an achievement goal. For example, you are working to get there.

In my town, it is very easy and expected to get bullied by others, but sometimes, that bully can hurt and make you want to quit your projects just because you don't want people laughing at you all the time; this can also be called dream killers. If you grow up in a town where people are like that, you better be prepared to support all this and have the courage to follow your dreams no matter what else happens.

After my second try to go to college, I wondered if there was something else I could do to increase my chances other than studying more. I found that omega three can help your brain retain more information and make the brain work better. I looked for some food that could have omega three, and tuna was one of them, so I was excited to try it and see its progress. Two months before the test, I decided to eat one can of tuna per day, and I told my sister about it; she was excited for me and my new method of improving myself; she offered to buy tuna for the first week and when she went to buy it, some questions were brought up, why are you buying too much tuna, are you going to make a tuna salad and you didn't invite me? One of her best friends asked this question. My sister was innocent when she thought sharing this purpose with her best friend would be a good idea. My sister responded, no, this is for my brother because he needs more omega 3 to retain more information so he can pass the entry test at the college, then her friend responded he thinks this is going to work.? I think he is crazy. I worked at the same company that my sister's friend's husband did. The next day, when all the workers and the owner had a break at work, this guy in front of everyone just asked me, Hey, Geo, did you bring your tuna here to make your brain work better? You might need to know what you are doing here because I don't see you focusing on the job. He laughed so hard that the other workers and the owner laughed. Then the owner said hold on but give us more details. This guy was carefully explaining to them my purpose for eating tuna, and they were laughing so hard at me that I didn't want to cry in front of them but was very close to doing so. I felt awful that I went. I got home. I asked my sister why she was sharing this with others, and she told me she had just told her best friend. I told my sister what happened at the job, and she felt pretty bad also, but I told her that in situations like this, we need to keep our mouths shut because people are dream killers.

I only tried eating tuna for one day, and after people laughed so hard at me, I decided not to try it anymore. I did the test, and I didn't pass, but I'll never know if this would have been different if I had followed what I thought was good to achieve my achievement goal.

Dear reader, this situation happens more often than we think. Now that you are reading this don't let people make you give up on what you think will work to achieve your goals in life. If people laugh at you and your dreams, then change that to an act of courage to conquer all your achievements.

YOUR ACHIEVEMENTS 2

Can your achievements generate jealousy in others, even those you never thought they would? Well, the answer is an inevitable yes. Be careful who you share your achievements with; perhaps they will make you feel bad because of that or because they couldn't get what you got by working hard for it.

My cousin and I grew up together; he is one year older than me, but we did everything together until we finished middle school. I remember some of our adventures as if they were yesterday. When we were about 12 and 13 years old, our aunt gave us a task where she would pay us some money if we went down the hill and grabbed seven sacks of rich soil for her flowers. This task would take us about 4 to 5 hours because the mountain was far away, and we could only get one sack at a time, but we decided to do it just for the adventure to see how many different animals we could see.

In the process, we saw a lot of animals, some of them very poisonous, like rattlesnakes and dangerous lizards, but we just oversaw them and avoided them; sometimes, we pranked each other, saying hey, there is a rattlesnake next to you don't move a muscle, then we frost immediately, and after a couple of seconds we start laughing and say gotcha! Knowing that it was just a prank, and we both laughed. After a few hours, we finished the last sack and were ready to get the money from our aunt. I decided to take my t-shirt off and start blowing cold air in my back; we did that a lot of times, and it felt excellent, but this time, the first time my shirt touched my back, I felt like someone gave me a whip. I thought it was just because my back was sweaty, so I gave myself a couple more, but every time, I felt like whipping myself. When I checked my T-shirt, I saw a (Lonomia obliqua caterpillar) dear reader. You can check that on the internet to get goosebumps, but I noticed that my back almost immediately was getting hives. However, my cousin laughed so hard at me because I did that. 20 years later, we were still talking and laughing about that time.

After I left Mexico, I visited my cousin a few times, and I thought he was happy that I was doing well in the United States, as I was when he talked to me about what he was doing well in Mexico. We talked about how each other was doing, and I told him about my achievements. Hey cousin, I learned English. I can communicate very well in the U.S. Hey cousin, guess what? I went to school, and now I know how to install electrical wires in any house; hey cousin, I have a driver's license in the United States. We were sharing each other achievements until one day, he told me Hey, stop right now. I am tired of you hearing what you are doing in the United States; you and I are different; we are from other worlds now; look at you; either you are blessed or cursed. I don't know which one yet, but I think you are cursed; I believe you sold your soul to the devil, everything was given to you, everything is very easy for you because you are lucky and I am not, so I don't want to hear any more what you are doing there is that clear?. I almost cried when I heard he thought everything was easy for me, but he wasn't there when I had to move alone. He wasn't there when I couldn't ask for the food I wanted, and I had to eat what the person in front of me was ordering even if I didn't like it because I couldn't ask for what I wanted. He wasn't there when I had no one to talk to about how I was feeling lonely, and he wasn't there to know that there was no luck. Still, there are sacrifices and hard work, and he wasn't there to understand that each of us fabrics our luck by making a lot of sacrifices and supporting a lot of pain that most people are scared to do. But I learned a lesson from this: no matter how close you are to someone; they might not feel excited about your achievements. Sometimes, it is better to keep it to yourself.

YOUR ACHIEVEMENTS 3

Keeping your achievements close and your mouth shut is humble. When you celebrate self-promotion, there is a constant need for validation, and you want to let others know how great you are, but the truth is that nobody will care about how high you get unless, somehow, they benefit as well. Humility is a virtue that encourages individuals to recognize their strengths and successes while remaining modest and unassuming. People can find you arrogant if you always talk about yourself, so if you want to keep a healthy environment at work and close friends, be careful how you express your achievements.

Competitions can sometimes inspire but can also lead to unhealthy comparisons and a bad competitive atmosphere. When individuals constantly discuss their success, it may create an environment where others feel compelled to measure up, potentially fostering resentment or envy.

One of my most significant achievements so far is when I joined the U.S. military in 2020, right after COVID-19 happened, but not all people thought this was a good idea. I have always admired soldiers worldwide because they put their lives upfront to defend their countries and loved ones, no questions asked. One day I was in a shopping store buying some clothes when suddenly it started to shake, a lot of people panicked, including myself, because I thought it was going to be a big earthquake. Quickly, some U.S. soldiers that were around started to give us directions so that we would not panic and to keep calm while we moved to a safer place. Immediately, people began to follow his instructions, and everyone became more relaxed because we felt protected by him. At that moment, I knew that I wanted the people around me to feel protected, also and I wanted to be an American soldier; when I shared this with my family, many of them were not happy, especially some uncles and aunts who tried to convince my mom and dad that joining the military was a bad idea, they said something like don't let Geo join the military, they have to use drugs to keep the hard training. Once they try this drug, they get addicted. When my mom brought this idea to me, I asked her if she knew someone in the military who could confirm this idea, but she replied no, I don't. Then, when my mom saw what I learned in the military, she was very happy that I joined. I told my mom not to believe other people's words if they had never experienced something in person and not to believe everything. Rumors and theories are easy to share, but keeping our mouths shut about something we don't know is difficult. We will talk more about this in chapter 9.

Dear reader, this is the activity for this chapter:

Put the names of three people you admire and ask them for one piece of advice that changes their lives; after the name, put the advice they give you. Then, put the names of your three favorite writers, singers, actors, or scientists, or combine those still alive. Write them a letter and ask them for advice on how to be successful like them in their area. You will experience excitement talking to people from different perspectives.

1.

2.

3

YOUR ACHIEVEMENTS 4

Going to school can be expected for some people but different for others. For me, it was complicated going to school where the only language spoken was English because I couldn't understand anything for almost six months.

In the United States of America, there are a lot of great programs that can help you succeed if you have the courage and decision it takes to do it. One of these most fantastic programs is a school called Job Corps, which is the most extensive nationwide career program to help young people from 14 to 24 years old; it allows people to finish high school education and trains them for meaningful careers also when they graduate, these team can help you to find an excellent job in your home town or wherever you decide to move.

In 2013, I had this great opportunity when one of my friends told me about where I could learn English and, at the same time, have a meaningful career. I initially chose an electrician for my job, which was complicated because of the language barrier. Still, I was learning English, and every day, I understood more and more. I told my friends about this school, but they told me I was crazy that there was no such a program that offered all these great things for free. When I insisted, they told me to focus on finding a good job and not bother other people who were looking for a better future; they said to me that I envied them because I didn't speak English, and now, I was trying to bring them down to the same level I was, that is when I understand that I had to keep my f mouth shut when nobody is asking me for help or I could ruin a good friendship.

Meanwhile, when I was in the Job Corps program, some opportunity to go after electrical training was right next to us; we could choose between underground and solar panels. Three friends and I were selected to go to an advanced program in Puerto Rico for solar panel training that took about eight months to finish. Still, we faced a problem: the program in Puerto Rico had already started, and they could not accept more students for the next few months. By that time, we would have finished the program at Job Corps and probably never had the chance to go for this program again. We tried to communicate with the school directors in Puerto Rico, but it was only through email because of the time difference, and we had only one week to get accepted or denied; we received one email per day, which didn't help us at all, the third day our advisor told us that was impossible to get ready for that program, we had no time and no experience to go on time. A friend and I discussed what "impossible" means; it is possible from the inside or "I'm- possible," so we part from there. We started collecting all the projects we needed to finish the program and all the signatures to be legitimate. After that, because we were told not to communicate with the school in Puerto Rico, we searched for the director's phone number and called them more than a few times until they answered. We talked to the director and explained that we wanted to get into the solar program, the future energy we wanted to be part of. After they spoke to each of us, they decided that they were going to give us a try and let us enter the program, but this almost got canceled because we couldn't keep our mouths shut right away after we talked to the directors in PR we went and told our supervisor that we contact them. Still, she was very mad. She told us that we couldn't do that, that she had already told us that we couldn't enter the program. She tried to cancel us, but we were lucky our instructor was a great person. She talked to the directors of our school and explained to them that we would be the first transfer students from this program, which could open the door for future students. They liked that we were in the school paper news that day. But remember that in critical situations that can change your life or give you a better opportunity, you have to be very selective when you open your mouth because this could change the whole situation.

YOUR ACHIEVEMENTS 5

People usually want you to do something all the time. Time is one of our most treasured gifts; family, health, and patience are others.

School was one of the most stressful parts of my life, especially during college. I found a part-time job during college as an apprentice electrician at the school; if I had two hours between classes, I worked those two hours and then returned to class. I felt like school time never ended because if I was not at work, I was at classes or had enough homework, even on the weekends. When I felt like I was catching up, exams were around the corner, so I had to study at night. Sometimes, I tried to study on Saturday all day, but after 8 hours, I got nothing done, just thinking I had an exam the following Monday.

I was looking for different learning methods. People learn in other ways, such as reading, watching or practicing, and writing. I decided to try them, and I wanted to write a study guide before the exam so that I could study them.

I had 12 writing pages for some classes, so I rewrote four pages to create a study guide and then studied from there. If I had an exam on Tuesday, I would have given myself three days to complete the guide, but when I started on Saturday for 6 or 7 hours, I just got 1 page done, and the other two days just passed. I don't know how many of you feel like that in school, but it is terrible.

People around me don't know how it feels to be under that pressure. I would give up college one semester before finishing because the pressure was too much, and I thought I couldn't handle it anymore, but somehow, I finished with some professor's help. Many people around me wondered when I would start working when I graduated because uncles and family members couldn't wait for me to start working. I had to tell at my graduation party that I would take four months off before I began looking for a job to relax a little bit after I accomplished my goal of graduating from college. Everyone would be happy to hear that, but it was the opposite. Family members and friends told my parents right away that they shouldn't pay for food or any bills for me now that I graduated and that I needed to start looking for a job immediately and putting money into buying a house. Also, I had to start paying for my student loans. I thought that next time I think someone will agree with my decisions about my life, I should keep my f mouth shut because they, instead of being happy, can complicate things even more.

YOUR FEELINGS 1

"The deepest feelings always show themselves in silence."

– MARIANNE MOORE

HAPPY

Have you ever heard the phrase don't promise when you are happy? Well, this is true; I'm guessing the creator of this phrase knew the significance of that phrase, and it is because a promise is something you are willing to complete no matter what. Emotions can make us feel different at the moment, and sometimes, if we are happy, we can promise something that we cannot complete later, but it seems it will be straightforward.

When I was in basic training in the military, I tried to focus only on finishing whatever tasks the drill sergeants told me to so I would not get into trouble or put my battle bodies in trouble. The days were very long; we woke up at 4 or 5 in the morning and started getting ready right away to do some exercise that sometimes lasted until 6:30 am. Then we went to breakfast. It was the best part of the day because breakfast was always delicious; after we took a shower to get ready for the day, it felt like we finished the day around 7:30 am, but the truth was that the day was only getting ready to start. This routine was every day except on weekends when we had two hours more to sleep.

I thought it would always be like that, but then I started meeting people who would be my friends forever, no matter what. I was shocked when I met a professional MMA fighter in my unit. She was very popular, and everyone went around her to ask her how what life was like as a skilled fighter. She was nice when I met her; I knew we would be good friends. I was happy to ask her more questions, and she would show me how life is in her world, so I promised her that when we got out of the basic training, I would visit her. I am from Minnesota, and she is from California, almost on the other side of the country, so I wasn't thinking clearly when I made her this promise. We got out, and I had to go back to college when her birthday was a week before it happened. I just said to her, sorry, friend, but I won't make it to your birthday this year, she replied I knew it, and now I know that your word means nothing. That was it. We have stopped talking since then.

Dear reader, if you are happy, think carefully before you open your mouth to make a promise. You can lose a perfect friend like I did because I didn't keep my mouth shut. So don't promise when you are happy.

YOUR FEELINGS 2

SAD

Sadness is a feeling when you don't want to talk with anybody. You might listen to sad music, stay in your room, and sometimes cry. This could happen for many reasons, but whatever the reason is, you don't want to tell anybody about it.

Where I grew up, people bully others constantly, and you have to learn how to live with that; age doesn't matter. As long as there is no physical bullying, it is ok for everyone. Most of the time, I was laughing and happy, but when I was sad, I didn't tell anyone; if people in my town knew that I felt bad or were unhappy, they would use that again to make me feel worse. This might sound like the wrong town to live in, but it is pretty good because it is a tiny town with around five thousand people. People will help you with no questions; they are very kind. I suppose bullying is a regular thing between friends, although sometimes they don't know that the bully they hurt.

Who doesn't like to hang out with friends? I used to do everything with friends; we went to concerts, parties, and school together. This changed for me when I got a girlfriend because now my time was with her instead of my friends. Although I wanted to spend more time with friends, it wasn't straightforward for me to choose. Well, I was always with my girlfriend, and my friends used to bully me when they passed by. I was with her; they yelled at me, saying Hey, Geo, we will see you at the party tonight after you leave there, and my girlfriend was just wondering what was happening. I told her that they did this thing to bully me. When we broke up, I was sad, and I thought it was a good idea to talk to my friends about it; they would find out sometime anyway, but what they did to me hurt even more every time we passed by her house, they yell at her house hey! Geo is here and wants to talk to you, but this wasn't true. I felt horrible and scared to pass by her house with friends because they made me feel awkward. Some people say your true friends are those you can bully and do anything with and still be friends with. I think that is true. If you have friends like mine, you should keep your mouth shut.

YOUR FEELINGS 3

ANGRY

Fallings sometimes can be against us if we let them manipulate the situation and we act without thinking.

Anger is one of the most dangerous feelings because it is when we can act more aggressively with people or say things we don't mean. We don't think about it and act. Our brain stops working logically and tells us to act by instinct to survive whatever situation we are in and defend ourselves right now.

When you get angry, that is one of the best moments to keep your f mouth shut because you might regret what you said, but it could be too late to fix it. This happened to my brother, who got an excellent job where he could learn precious skills detailing houses from inside and outside. That was a hard job to get because people usually ask for some experience, and just very few are willing to teach you the job from the beginning; sometimes, the employers risk the time that you will leave the job once you know everything and maybe you will be competition to the company. My brother agreed on a start salary, and everything was good. He was starting to get more experience and started doing more responsibilities, and after a while, they agreed on a raise for the salary. After some time, another worker started the same job, and now it was three people, including my brother. One day, the employer told my brother to go to finish a job with his coworker. They were working when the house owner told them how much the employer was charging for each of them, and this caused some questions between my brother and his coworker; they were wondering if they should talk to their employer and ask them about the difference that he was charging for them. One day, they spoke to their employer and said something like this: hey, we talked to the owner of the house you sent us, and he told us how much you were charging for us, and we want the rest of the money; the employer was not in a good mood and looked at them and told them, I am paying you what we agreed before and if you don't like it, you can leave today. Well, my brother and his coworkers were not in a good mood either, and they said OK, if that is what you want, we will do that since tomorrow we are not coming to work. Some suitable lessons happened here: my brother shouldn't open his mouth that way because his employer was paying him what they agreed, and the rest should not be my brother's business; whatever his employer charges for him should not matter because that is his business, not my brother's. Another thing that happened was that my brother lost a good job where he was learning good skills because he didn't keep his mouth shut.

YOUR FEELINGS 4

FEAR

When you have fears, it is better not to tell anyone, mainly because talking about them is like admitting that something scared you. It becomes more realistic, which could make you feel more scared.

As kids, sometimes people and even our parents try to scare us if we don't do something they want, like eating our vegetables or going to bed early.

When we were kids, my cousin and I used to scare each other with creepy stories that we heard from people or sometimes created ourselves to scare each other. We had a bigger cousin who always sat with us, and she liked it when we went to her house, which was a 10-minute' walk from our house. At night, when we were at her house listening to her stories, we begged her to come with us because if she didn't, something terrible would happen to us after hearing her stories. She liked to use some magical things that happened in our town or close to it. Let's see some of them. She started: Hey, did you hear what happened to the men living in the greenhouse next to my house? No, we didn't hear anything. This guy was looking for treasure in the mountain, and there was a cave. People told him that whatever he did, he should never enter the cave, but this guy did it, and guess what happened? What tells us what happened? Well, he found a treasure, but when he tried to get it, some elves came, and they told him this treasure is yours, but we want something from you. We want two kids, bring them, and all this treasure is yours. Guys, this guy is looking for the two kids the elves ask for, and the kids have to be around your age, so if you see this guy, don't get close to him because he will take you to the elves, and you will never come back. After hearing this story, my cousin and I couldn't get to our house alone because we were afraid of this man. One day, I told my cousin what kind of things I fear more, and he told his sister and his sister told our bigger cousin, so she used this thing to scare us more. Sometimes, we even started crying until she helped us to get home safely. Occasionally, we are afraid of things, but if you don't want people to use this against you someday, dear reader, it is better to keep your mouth shut.

YOUR FEELINGS 5

ANXIETY

When you feel anxiety can be harmful, you have the feeling that you have to get somewhere quickly, but you don't even know why. If you are driving, you want to reach the destination but don't know why. Sometimes, you feel like you have to solve other people's problems.

My mom always said that it is better to avoid any argument and always tried to solve the problems in our family. My mom has five siblings, and she acts like the judge sometimes between their difficulties. One day, two of her sisters, Sophia and Margarita, the oldest and youngest, argued about Margarita's daughters, Raquel and Karol. My aunt Sophia was telling my mom that Raquel had taken some clothes from her house and she hadn't returned yet; my mom asked her if you had seen her take my aunt said no, but she was the only one enter the house that day that it get lose so my mom told her no Raquel didn't look it was Karol. I know it was Karol because she also took some of the clothes for my daughter and hasn't returned them yet. My aunt Sophia told my mom, "OK, you know who did it. You tell Margarita who did it so you can fix the problem; my mom didn't do it. Then, rumors spread that my mom was saying something about her nieces. After that, my aunt Sophia and Margarita were mad at my mom. They didn't talk to her for a while because my mom was trying to solve problems that didn't correspond to her.

I think my mom should tell my aunt Sophia right away that if she was suspected of something, she should go and talk directly to the person she suspected and not get involved with others. Maybe if she did that, the problem wouldn't be that big.

YOUR FEELINGS 6

PRIDE

Usually, parents feel proud of their sons when they achieve anything, like finishing high school, getting a college degree, or getting married. Sometimes, they like to share this feeling with others, thinking they will also see it that way.

My dad sometimes tells me how proud he feels of me for doing something, but he does it even when I ask him not to share what I did with others. But sometimes, when I see these people that my dad talked to about me, they come to me and tell me something like hey, Geo, why do you walk that way? Why do you think you are better than us just because you did what your dad told us? I'll let you know what, Geo, you are not superior to us, so don't walk like that in front of me, ok? I was speechless when I heard stuff like that because I didn't even try to walk differently; after listening to this from one family member, I tried to walk normally around him and ended up walking more awkwardly. I told my dad not to say stuff to people because not all of them would see it as my dad does.

Dear reader, this is the activity for this chapter.

Let's play the best-motivated song for 15 minutes, you know, then write down three goals for the end of the year that came to mind right after that. Some famous people say if you think you can achieve a goal in one year, it will take you one year, but if you have the same goal, it will take you three months, then it will take you three months, so don't procrastinate your goals and start today.

YOUR FEELINGS 7

HELP

If you can help someone, don't tell them you will. Keep your mouth shut and help someone without communicating this, especially to the people you are trying to help. Let's check this story, which shows the truth and how your words can hurt others even if you try to help them.

On a cold night, a rich guy found a poor older man who didn't have any place to go or to sleep; the rich man asked him, aren't you cold outside without any coat? The older man responds, yes, I am out without a coat, but I am used to it. Then the rich man said, wait here for me. I am going inside my house and will bring you a nice warm coat. The older man was pleased and said yes, Sr. I will be waiting for you here. The rich man enters his house and starts doing stuff that he didn't complete, and he forgets about the older man. The following day, he remembered the older man, and he went outside to find him, but he found him dead from the cold, but in his hands, the older man had a note. "When I didn't have warm clothes, I had the strength to fight against the cold because I was used to it, but when you promised to help me, I clung to your promise, and that took away my power of resistance."

Dear reader, can you tell the moral of this story? "don't promise anything if you cannot make it; it might not be anything to you, but it could be everything to someone else."

By this point, you will learn that it is better sometimes to be silent and that not everything needs to be said. Also, silence is better than unnecessary drama. If you can avoid unnecessary drama, your life and relations will improve. When you get your feelings on top, think about what you will say before you say it. You don't want to say something that could bring you problems later.

YOUR DREAMS 1

'You learned the three greatest things in life: Never say everything you know and

keep your mouth shut."

Sometimes, we want to communicate something, but we miscommunicate. When you are working on your dreams and finding the person who can help you build them, you have to be careful about sharing your ideas because if you use the wrong words, that person who could help you might run away. You won't have another chance to talk to the person, so if you are not ready to communicate your dream ideas correctly, it is better to keep your mouth shut.

This is one story from a king and those who can interpret dreams. The king one day had a dream where he lost all his teeth, so he asked one of the king's advisors what to do; the advisor told him to call the guy who can interpret dreams, so that is what the king did. When the guy arrived at the kingdom, the king told him about his dream; I dream that I lost all my teeth. Tell me what this means. After thinking for a bit, the guy said, my king, I have bad news for you; your dream means that you will see how all your family died individually. The king didn't like this interpretation, and he told one of the guards to bring this guy outside and execute him. After that, the king asks for another guy who can interpret dreams, and the king tells him his dream; the dream interpreter thinks for a little bit, and he tells the king. Your majesty, I have great news for you: your dream means that you will live longer than all your family. The king thought briefly and told one of the guards to bring this man outside and give him 60 gold coins. If we analyze the two men, they gave the king the same interpretation; why was one of them executed and the other rewarded? It was simple: one talked about death, and the other spoke about life. Both answers correspond to the same interpretation, but we must be like the second man and talk wisely when communicating our ideas and dreams.

I like to gamble, and one of my dreams is to have a casino one day; this idea was not ready yet, and I didn't think about it when I shared it with someone who could help me get the connections to open a casino. My mentor, who was also my professor in college, has always encouraged me to follow my dream and that anything is possible; you need to meet the right people and go from there. I have a perfect relationship with this professor, and he helped me with some of the crazy ideas I have that don't sound too crazy to him. I decided to share this casino idea with him like this. Professor, I am working on some designs for a casino close to Utah (in Utah, the casinos are illegal). I want to provide all kinds of accommodations for customers, like a swimming pool, bars for drinks, nice hotel rooms, a toco restaurant with Mexican recipes, and a great environment where people can go and spend their money. Everything was good until I said, "Where people expend their money." Then, the professor asked me more questions about the idea, and my answers didn't convince him that this was a good idea. He told me that all your ideas before were about helping people. It appears you are looking for something where people can go, and why not ruin their lives? I cannot help you with this idea, and I cannot recommend any of my contacts for your idea. I wouldn't be happy knowing I helped someone whose idea is to take advantage of others. Some advice is: "Don't marry with one idea because this might not be the best idea, which is also okay." After that, we didn't talk as much as before, and I reflected that I was very excited when I shared this with him. I didn't even think about the power of the words that could come from my mouth. My original idea was to build a place where people could have a great time and forget about work and stress for some weekends so they could go back to work fresh and full of exciting moments they had with their friends and family. I made it sound different because I didn't study the situation before speaking. That is why now if I want to share a dream or idea, I first keep my mouth shut and then reflect on how I will share it with the right people when I have the right moment to do it.

YOUR DREAMS 2

Sometimes, we want to share other dreams with others; these are the ones we want to pursue, and we think other people will benefit from the same path, and we want to encourage them to follow us or do the same thing we are doing. This happened to me when I was going to start school, and I wanted some of my cousins to join me, but they didn't have the same perspective about that school that I did; in this case, it would be better for me to keep my mouth shut instead tried to convince them that it was an excellent opportunity for them also.

When I had just come to the United States, one opportunity knocked on my door: to go to school where I could learn a trade like an electrician, and at the same time, I was going to learn English. Everything was for free at some school government association called Job Corps. This, for me, was a formidable opportunity, and I wanted to share it with some of my cousins who have been here for around nine years. Still, they told me that such a school didn't exist here, that this must be some trick or fake information I got from somebody. I shared the idea with three cousins living in different states. All three got me the same conclusion; one of them told me, you go ahead and let me know when you are actually in the school, but until then, don't bother me with some stupid dreams and fantasies that you have in your mind, keep that bullshit to yourself. Once I was at the school, I tried again to reach out to my cousins, and I wanted to convince them to join me, saying that it was real and they could also benefit from it. Another one told me; I am making more money than you would once you leave your stupid school. The last one told me; I know English already; I have been here for more years than you. Do you think I have been wasting my time like you are doing right now in that school? Maybe in the future, you will have better things to do than waste your time. All the answers they gave me was for me to leave them alone; they would not be engaging in school or hearing my great stories; the truth is that they didn't care at all for anything that I was doing, and the better thing for me to do was to keep my mouth shut and do what I believe was good for me but do this quietly.

YOUR DREAMS 3

I am sure many of us dream someday of having a business where we can be our bosses and choose our work schedules. I had this dream when I was 12 years old, but since I didn't have any income, it wasn't easy to start building something. It was not until I was 17 that I started gaining some income, but I had other possessions that could provide me money, like a gold chain that I could sell for cash.

My brother sold me this change one day, and I wanted to start something, so I saw the opportunity to start something by myself. When I sold the chain, I bought a pressure washer machine to start a car wash in my town. When my mom asked me what happened to the chain and I explained to her why I sold it, she was mad; she told me that she would buy it for me but I told her that I wanted to do something for myself and that it was my investment and my risk to start a business and I wanted to decide by myself. My aunt was listening to the conversation, and no matter what I said or explained to my mom, I made her understand that my idea was complicated. The more I talked, the more confused she was. At this point, I should have kept my mouth shut and not explained more because the conversations were getting scary with questions like do you owe money to somebody? Are you in some illegal business that I should know of? Then, my aunt told my mom that I was getting crazy. The things I said, like I wanted to start a business, didn't make sense to my aunt, and she told my mom that I was hiding something more significant and for sure I was using drugs. But I learned that sometimes if you cannot explain your idea to someone and you are not going anyway, it is better to let the other person talk and agree with them; the best thing for us is to keep our f mouth shut and tell the person who is trying to change our mind that we appreciate their opinion and we are going to take what there are telling us in consideration.

YOUR DREAMS 4

People will always tell you what you can and cannot do, but the reality is that they will give you their opinion based on what they feel capable of, not what you are capable of. When you share a dream, be careful about what you are listening to, and don't let other people's opinions get in your way of achieving your dreams; if people tell you that it is impossible to do, tell yourself it is impossible until somebody does it, "if somebody did it already so I can and if nobody did it yet, I'd be the first one to do it."

I had some brilliant friends. His name is Robert, and since we were kids, he has always had some good explanations for everything and some gist to explain things the way a scientist would. I could trust him to tell him anything, and he would find some way to make things, ideas, and projects happen, or at least that is what I thought. When we are kids, there is no limit to our dreams; we can be anything, we can fly, we can have superpowers, we can visit the stars, and we don't think of danger or the impossible; we just in our minds are the best superheroes that ever exist. Albert Einstein said, "Imagination is more important than knowledge." If we could keep that mentality, I think people would be happier, and jobs would be better for everyone because we would be doing what makes us happy. For this reason, our jobs would be better performed, and our lives would be so much better.

I liked watching the stars and dreaming that I was a superhero and could fly worldwide. I discussed this with my friend Robert; he always thought flying might be possible. One day, I had an idea: to write a book. When I told Robert about my idea, he laughed and said I couldn't write a book. He told me that I have to study a lot of grammar, punctuation, and pronunciation. He said that it would be impossible for me because I had not been born to write a book because my grades in literature and the amount of money that I have to put into a project like this would be immense, and I would probably not see this money in my whole life. I had never seen him talking more seriously before, and because he was more intelligent than me, I had to believe what he was saying. Plus, he ensured I understood what he was trying to communicate, and I should never talk about this idea anymore. After he told me everything about why I would never be able to write a book and make sure I understood, I just laughed and said to him that I was joking and that I knew writing a book would be impossible for someone like me, and I told myself that I would keep my f mouth shut for my dreams. Instead, I would work in silence to pursue them. I almost believed what Robert told me that day, but then I decided to give it a try at something that I was scared to do.

Twenty years later, after Robert told me I would never write a book, I decided to do it anyway; this is a book with no experience in writing, a book for the people who want to take action and do things with no experience, people who don't want to wait for the perfect moment to do things and pursue dreams. Dream big and start working for your dreams today; the ideal moment to plan your dreams is today; start where you are and what you have right now.

"Somebody with less talent, contacts, money, and possibilities than you are doing your dream job right now."

Dear reader, start working on your dreams now. Write down some projects, ideas, and dreams you want to achieve in a blank notebook, put a due date for each, and start working on them today. You don't have to quit your job or give up anything; find 30 minutes daily to work on that notebook.

This is the activity and last activity for this book. Dear reader, hang on your wall your dreams so that you can see them when you wake up and before you go to sleep, then promise yourself that you are going to work on those dreams no matter what is your actual situation, even if you are scared to do it or someone told you already that your dream is impossible for you. Work 30 minutes from Monday to Friday until you achieve them individually. When you reach the first, use that inspiration to help others do the same thing for theirs. And that is all for this activity.

YOUR DREAMS 5

If you dream of traveling, don't tell anyone. It's better to post pictures in a different place; people will make fun of you if you tell them you want to go to Paris or Tokyo.

This happened to me again because I didn't know how to keep my mouth shut, and I thought people or friends would encourage me to travel, but instead, they laughed at me. Different accents depend on your state in Mexico; my first trip out of Mexico was to Jalisco when I was 14. My cousin married a girl from Jalisco anfd invited me to visit. When I was there and heard these people talking with a different accent, I was excited because I had never heard anything like that. I was there for five days, but those were the best vacations of my life at the time.

My cousins and I were playing to mimic the accent that we just heard a few days before. People in my town were making fun of us because we were trying to use different accents and talking with other words. When I told the people of my town that someday I would go to a different country, they didn't wait a minute to make fun of me; I heard things like, hey, you think because you went to a different city, you could go to a different country? Are you out of your mind? The sun must hurt your brain. Do you know how much money you need to travel to the city you went to? Do you even know how to work to make money? If you want to travel, you have to save money for about 30 years. Geo, don't be stupid. Take this vacation like something you might do every five years.

Hearing all these things was like traveling; knowing how these people make sounds must be challenging. Seven years later, I moved to the United States, and even here, people were telling me that just because I was living in the USA, I didn't even think travel would be easy. My first country to visit after the USA was Japan; then people told me that I was lucky that my parents paid for all these things, but they didn't know that they didn't pay for my trip; I was paying for it, then I visited four countries in Europe Italy, France, Portugal, and Spain. When I traveled to these countries, I was in college, and I had a part-time job where I could save money during school and travel on school vacations. Then I went to more countries like Colombia, Canada, and Guatemala, and people from my town started asking me for souvenirs, pictures, and advice on how to travel.

Dear reader, don't wait too long if you plan to travel. Take the vacations you want, go to different palaces, meet new people, and eat different authentic food. The worst that can happen if you travel is that you won't like to be in one place anymore; you would like to be moving around, and even that is a win, so don't wait too long. Just remember to Keep Your Mouth Shut.

"People will laugh at you first, then question you, and then ask you how can they also do it."

www.ingramcontent.com/pod-product-compliance
Lightning Source LLC
Chambersburg PA
CBHW050314230526
45471CB00005B/2179